EBURY PRESS

# RITUALS OF A HAPPY SOUL

Deepanshu Giri is an engineer by profession and an established name in the world of underwater robotics. In 2017–18, he took a sabbatical to pursue his penchant for astrology. Deepanshu was born into a Brahmin family in the lineage of Lord Bhrigu. He is also blessed by his family, who have been into astrology and Ayurveda for the last seven generations.

In 2018, he started Lunar Astro Vedic Academy to share his learnings with other astrology lovers. His revolutionary approach to astrology has garnered a following that is unprecedented in such a short span of time. Since then, the Lunar Astro family has been growing by leaps and bounds. Students from across the globe and age groups have joined in, a testament to his vision of astrology.

Deepanshu has done a deep dive into astrology by decoding and simplifying the mystical texts and applying his research to put forth jaw-dropping, logic-defying, stunning predictions. Every year, he brings out unique research-based content on completely different subjects at Lunar Astro.

Lunar Astro Vedic Academy was set up to preserve India's ancient system of knowledge, especially Vedic astrology. Its research-based content is unmatched by any Vedic school online or offline. Students of Lunar Astro are trained and mentored in such a way that they are steadily turning into an army of professional astrologers and making a mark for themselves.

# ADVANCE PRAISE FOR THE BOOK

'Deepanshu takes us on a whirlwind tour—one that lies at the intersection of spirituality, universal science, astrology and philosophy—and helps us navigate a complex terrain, guiding us on how to connect to a source of "unlimited energy from the universe". . . . I delighted in reading it as Deepanshu's contribution to the ever-expanding genre of self-help books. This book is unequivocal, deals with no dilemma of jargon and is filled with real-life experiences to reinforce its teachings. Its purpose is not to preach but to let "several millions of people out there heal themselves by using the energy of the universe". Drawing from the Vedas, this book is critical, pragmatic and most of all, honest—offering practical insights on cultivating positivity, understanding the elements that shape our world and embracing gratitude. With the core message of "whatever goes around, comes around", this, here, is an indispensable guide on summoning good deeds and fortitude even in the face of adversity'—**Shashi Tharoor, member of Parliament (Thiruvananthapuram), Lok Sabha**

'This book is a captivating journey into the world of astrology that will resonate with both beginners and seasoned enthusiasts alike. Deepanshuji weaves together accessible explanations of complex astrological concepts with engaging anecdotes and real-life applications, making the material relatable and very enjoyable'—**U.U. Lalit, former chief justice of India**

# RITUALS
## OF A
# HAPPY
# SOUL

DEEPANSHU GIRI

EBURY
PRESS

An imprint of Penguin Random House

EBURY PRESS

Ebury Press is an imprint of the Penguin Random House group of companies
whose addresses can be found at global.penguinrandomhouse.com

Published by Penguin Random House India Pvt. Ltd
4th Floor, Capital Tower 1, MG Road,
Gurugram 122 002, Haryana, India

First published in Ebury Press by Penguin Random House India 2025

ISBN 9780143475491

Typeset in Sabon LT Std by Manipal Technologies Limited, Manipal
Printed at Thomson Press India Ltd, New Delhi

www.penguin.co.in

# Contents

# CONTENTS

# The Best Part About Believing in Magic Is:

## IT HAPPENS

The secret about energy is that everything around us has energy. This book also has energy, as a result of which the moment you start reading it you will experience a trance-like energy. You will feel the energy of joy, which will make you feel like dancing, as this was the energy I felt while writing this book.

There are so many inexplicable things that will happen to you while reading this book. Each time you pick up this book, an unexpected call or a knock on the door or something very unusual will happen. This is because the moment you start reading this book, your thoughts and vibrations are going to attract energy towards you.

There is energy around you that will let you feel its presence by the breaking of certain objects or electrical gadgets suddenly malfunctioning. All this is nothing but energy trying to communicate with you to make sure you feel the presence of all visible and invisible beings. Instead of being afraid, communicate with energy and let the universe know that you are open to learning this magic. Raise both your arms several times in the air while reading and you will feel the bliss.

If things are normal with you and you don't see unexpected things happening to you by the end of the book, then email me and say that magic doesn't work for you, and I will accept it. But since I know how powerful energy is, email me your experiences at happyrituals108@gmail.com or write to me on my Facebook page or the Lunar Astro website.

This may be new to some of you, but don't be afraid. Energy is there to help you grow in life so that you can feel the bliss of the universe. I always write books during the period between Mahashivratri and Holi, when the universe is charged with so many vibrations. I feel the cosmos is pouring nectar on earth. I wish to pass on the same energy to all of you so that you can experience the power of the universe.

# Rituals of a Happy Soul:

# NOT A SPIRITUAL BOOK

Warning: This is not a spiritual book, as I am someone who is far away from spirituality of any kind. Spirituality asks you to accept situations as they come and not react to any situation. Spirituality is what the Buddha preaches to become one with nature by mastering the art of ignoring the problems in life.

This is a book to awaken the hidden energy inside you so that you can overcome all your problems and enjoy success in this life. This is a book that teaches you about the magic of the universe that lies within you. It is only self-doubt inside you that has made you stop believing in magic. Your brain has been programmed to limit your capabilities, so you forget your true worth.

The book contains several rituals to harness energy that have no relation to religion of any kind. Religion binds you through rules. Religion is always taken over by fanatics for their own benefit, leaving no scope for free thinking. This is the main reason for the downfall of religion in any society. This is a book of universal science, which we were supposed to learn while growing up. But this knowledge was suppressed so that other agendas could be promoted for the benefit of a few powerful people. When I worked on a ship alongside people of different nationalities, and I got to know about the cultural backgrounds of other people, it was apparent to me that rituals all over the world are carried out with the same intention, although the process may vary.

In India, when a child is sick, the grandmother performs a small ritual to ward off any negative energy that has attacked the child. My Egyptian friend Maged al-Hosny used to do the same thing with our submarine when it would break down. It worked like magic! In fact, in both countries, this is called *nazar* or evil eye.

In India, when I used to enter my home, my wife would pour some oil on the side of the door to remove any negative energy that I could be carrying with me. Similarly, when I would leave my office in Tehran, a wonderful lady would sprinkle some water on me and my bag and recite an *ayat* to make my journey smooth and easy like water.

The whole purpose of rituals is to make your life more comfortable and easier by getting an abundance of energy from the universe. It is to make you more powerful and take care of any negative energy that is coming your way. All the rituals we see in any religion were made for kings. A king had to stay in power and his decisions affected the whole country, so it was very important for kings to keep performing rituals.

This is a book about rituals, which will not only give you clear instructions on how to manage your energy but also how to connect to a source of unlimited energy from the universe.

# 1

## 'I Am Stuck'

I receive a lot of emails every day from different people asking for guidance and help. One of the common phrases I keep hearing is 'I am stuck'—I am stuck in a bad job, I am stuck in a marriage, I am stuck with bad health, or whatever the condition may be. While this is a common term that I read every day in my emails, no one is paying attention to *why* they are stuck.

At any point in time when you are stuck in your life, it is because of a lack of energy in life. Imagine a car trying to go through rough terrain and where there is a muddy patch, the car gets stuck. The car owner runs around blaming everyone else, saying that he has been stuck there for the past ten hours due to the muddy patch. He needs to realize that the problem is not the bad terrain but the low power of his car. The same patch can easily be conquered by a 4x4 truck as it has more power than a small car.

Similarly, problems in your life seem bigger when you are running low on energy. When you gain enough energy, any problem in life will seem smaller and more manageable. It is only because of your personal disconnect from energy that you are unable to handle the rough patches and get stuck in life. Problems in life will never end, so it is better to make yourself more powerful. You don't fall sick because of a virus, as viruses are always present inside. It is only when your immunity is low that the virus is able to make you fall sick. This is the principle of energy in life.

For me, it all started when I witnessed magic in real life. I had this experience when I was trying to decode several principles of astrology. Astrology is like a data science written 5000 years ago to solve human problems. It is like planet x at a particular position in the sky will produce the following results. It was very fascinating, but I wanted to go deeper into the subject. I was running from pillar to post, trying to find someone who could explain to me what I was searching for. Finally, it came to a point where I realized that no one was interested in learning the secrets of the cosmos. No one was questioning themselves. So, I started questioning myself and, instead of searching for answers outside and asking different people, I turned inwards and started looking for answers within. Thereafter, I started getting answers via an energy burst. What I mean by an energy burst is that I was attracting a lot of energies and inexplicable things began to happen. In the beginning, it was fascinating and then it came to a point when magic was a normal daily routine. It was like giving eyesight to a blind person.

I am writing this book so that each of you can experience the magic that this universe holds around you. You are ignoring this magic every day. Nature only gives us the energy that our body can handle. You need a body like a yogi to handle energy directly entering into the crown chakra. The headache you can get is so bad that no medicine will help until and unless your body absorbs it. That is why some people vomit or go to sleep just to absorb the energy.

Imagine if 4000 volts go into a circuit of 200 volts—a short circuit will happen. There is a picture of a yogi sitting under a tree with a spirit connection from his crown chakra to the top. For yogis it is fine, but if you are not elevated in terms of energy, please don't try this.

After I started experiencing so many subtle forms of energy while dealing with astrology, I decided to share some of these incidents via my blog, YouTube

channel and Facebook. I realized that I was not the only one who was getting the energy burst from the sky. Other people were having similar experiences. One of the reasons that subscribers were so connected with us was that I was sharing something that everyone could see take place in their daily lives. And even if they couldn't, then when people tried some simple energy manifestation exercises, they could see the results on their own.

This is a process of energy which cannot truly be described to anyone. How it feels when you place your tongue on a 9V battery cannot be described to someone until they experience the current in their own body. You will never be able to make them feel the same experience.

I will explain the process in detail in the book. As we progress through the chapters, you should try every single technique mentioned. It is a process and if anyone follows it, in the end, the result will be the same. You will be able to feel the bliss in your inner core.

# 2

# Why I Am Writing This

I am writing this book based on my practical experience of healing several clients and their testimonies. It is about how, using the energy of ragas, I experienced healing, and how I was able to decode several mysteries of astrology by experiencing domains and realms of the other world. I am introducing you to the energy realm of the universe. By following the step-by-step guide, you will be able to raise your energy levels to a point where you can see the magic happening in your life.

Everything around you is a form of energy—it can be a positive energy or a negative energy depending on what you are attracting by different means. We will discuss forms of energy by giving you an introduction to the various types, without using complicated words or processes. The purpose of this book is to let you experience the energy of different realms.

Let me give you a practical example. One morning, I saw a post in our group from Dr Subhro Chakraborty, from Kolkata, explaining how he is suffering from unbearable pain due to a condition called Ménière's disease. He was unable to drive due to vertigo and vomiting for the last ten years. As I was reading this, I could feel the pain in his words. I wondered why a human being had to suffer like this and be in such a bad condition, especially since he was a doctor who must be serving so many people in the world.

When he first asked for help in the group, a lot of people commented that he should go to a good doctor. But then he explained that he himself was a doctor and there was no cure for this disease in medical science anywhere in the world.

I recommended a simple remedy to him. I asked him to fast on a particular moon cycle and told him to recite particular hymns and to get back to me with his feedback. After a few weeks, this is the feedback he left on the Facebook link to the original message.

Gratitude and Unique Remedy success by Shri Deepanshu Giri*:

---

*  *https://www.facebook.com/groups/lunarastro/posts/10592867 44648171/*

Namaskar everyone. I am sharing a real-life experience of mine. My name is Dr Subhro Chakraborty, male, 46 years old. I am a Cardiologist (MBBS, MD Med, DM Cardiology) in Kolkata. The reason I have disclosed my professional degree is to tell you that I did all the degrees of medical science in India and am well versed with medicine.

I am a generally unhealthy person with multiple health issues from the second decade of my life and I have consulted many astrologers. I have tried remedies for my health issues. Some worked partially, some did not. I am suffering from a disease known as Meniere's disease of left ear for the last ten years that has made my life hell. This usually manifests as loud sound in one ear (tinnitus), ear fullness, severe vertigo with recurrent vomiting and fall attack. Medical science only has some symptomatic treatment for this. Believe me, I have tried everything, being a doctor with a lot of contacts here and even abroad but there was no satisfactory solution. I couldn't drive due to fear, hearing loss and my life is gradually becoming hell. Last November, I have put a post in the Lunar Astro group. Shri Deepanshu Giri has seen my problem and suggested a simple remedy . . . initially without seeing my chart and later on after seeing my chart.

The remedy worked like blessings in my life . . . I started doing it with full belief and gradually got relief from chronic tinnitus and vertigo . . . my medicines for Meniere's disease were almost off!

How can I thank Shri Deepanshu Giri who did a free reading in a group post and helped me to get rid of my most distressing problem . . . Please remember guys, some of the things we need to suffer for is our karma phal so I have asked about this which is bothering me the most! The link of my previous post is given here:*

I express my deep gratitude to Shri Deepanshu Giri (my healer, my guru) and all of the Lunar Astro faculty members, I love u all.

Hare Krishna, Hare Krishna, Krishna Krishna Hare Hare, Hare Ram, Hare Ram, Ram Ram, Hare Hare.

Dr Subhroo Chakrabborty (Subhro Chakraborty) MBBS MD Medicine

DM Cardiology

AFESC (Associate Fellow of European Society of Cardiology)

---

* *https://www.facebook.com/groups/lunarastro/permalink/1016956868881159/*

Assistant Professor in Cardiology North Bengal Medical College, Siliguri Residence: Kolkata

(My disclosures are given to show that I know modern medical science still I got immensely benefitted by the remedy of Akadasi fast).

What do you think happened in the case above? Do I have a magic wand like Harry Potter, or a crystal ball or a magic mirror? I was able to pull something off which medical science was not able to even in ten years. The person got relief by simple fasting. The only thing I initiated here was that I identified the problem and told him to connect with the energy source of the universe so that he could heal himself. On the eleventh lunar day, the energy is of healing, and on an empty stomach, energy can move with the least resistance in the body to heal diseases.

We will discuss fasting in detail in a separate chapter, but my aim is to make you heal. Like Dr Chakraborty, there will be many of you who may be taking medicines and still living in pain. I want you to understand that the universe wants you to heal; it is you who is not connecting yourself to the energy source to allow the healing process.

The purpose of this book is to let several millions of you out there heal yourselves by using the energy of the universe. As these are self-instructing methods, you will be able to get results from day one and start a new journey of your life. You will experience things which you have kept hidden so deep in your body that it has started to come out in the form of diabetes, OCD, autism, hormonal imbalance, depression, anger, etc.

In this book, we will start by identifying the issues and then gradually move on to how we can heal ourselves so that we become the best version of ourselves. This book will help you to become happy, compassionate and content in life. Once you achieve this, you will realize how much you can achieve by being the true happy version of yourself.

Any form of problem you have in your life at any moment is due to the *Shadripus*—the six types of enemies as explained in the Vedas. These six enemies live within us, creating trouble at various levels in our bodies. It will start with small issues on the mental plane, and later on, it will manifest as physical deformity and pain in our lives.

There are very few people who understand that the real cause of their suffering is within them. No one else can make you feel miserable or happy until and unless your inner core decides to feel that way. We feel happy or sad by looking at a certain place or feel miserable by someone's words. Those words remind us of memories that are not resolved completely and cause anger and pain. For instance, when you look at your ex-boss or ex-spouse in public and have some unresolved feelings, you will not feel comfortable with this interaction as they remind you of that pain that is still inside you.

When you see a person who is rude to everyone and always on edge and ready to burst into anger with anyone, at any time, this person is not disappointed with you. In fact, this person is disappointed with themself. Their own shortcomings come out in the form of anger towards other people.

It is always shortcomings and unresolved issues within us and the need to address any pain which we store, that causes the behaviour. There are things which we want to say to our spouse, parents, in-laws, boss and all those people who have hurt us, but we have kept them stored in our hearts, and then, we forget about them. Remember the pain is still inside and it will come back in some other form which we might not be aware of.

I am writing this book to make sure you address your pain in the right manner. By healing yourself you become the best version of yourself. In life, when you operate with a completely happy state of mind, there is no one better than you. During my consultations, I have felt the pain of several people who were not able to fix themselves after being damaged by loved ones, or who are unable to recover from broken dreams. This book is an attempt to give relief to each one of them.

# 3

# Attracting Energies

We attract different people into our lives as we continuously radiate energy. Look around you carefully. Where you are sitting and whatever condition you are in at present in your life, good or bad, is a result of your energy and of what you have attracted and allowed in your life. If we can attract different people into our lives, how much and how quickly can it work? You are the biggest transmitter to radiate energy 24/7. If your energy is scattered, or if your body is not ready to radiate above a certain level of energy, then you will get results according to your body—just as a 10W transmitter cannot perform the work of a 1000W transmitter. But the good thing is that with the help of continuous practice, you can increase your power.

You will feel some of the results within two days. Then you can start observing that when you think of someone in the morning, by the evening that person will call you. Or when you sing a song in your mind, that song will reach you somehow. This is the law of attraction, but it only works at the level on which you are vibrating. For instance, let us suppose someone's goal is to meet the president of the US, which has a high degree of unlikelihood—that much more time and continuous energy efforts are required for bigger goals like this. You can't have a goal of becoming a millionaire and then expect it to happen by evening. But if you continuously improve your energy and keep radiating the energy of money, it will happen.

## Your Own Engine

We all have a personal power engine inside us, just like it is in different vehicles. Say a person wants to travel 2000 km and decides to go on the journey on a bicycle. In one month, he might only be able to travel 400 km. According to him, whoever said that you can travel 2000 km in a few hours is a liar and it is not possible to cover this distance in less than six months. The problem is not in the distance but in the power applied by that person as he has chosen a bicycle, while someone else might have chosen a car or may even be travelling by jet. Similarly, we all have different capabilities based on our lifestyles and will experience results differently.

At any point in time, subconsciously, you choose things which are based on your thought patterns, and these decisions, small or big, decide the level of your life. As an example, think of your body as a receiver which has a particular bandwidth of frequency. Now, wherever you travel to in the world, you can only respond to this particular bandwidth of energy. Anything below this frequency or above this frequency will be something you can never understand in life.

Ninety-eight per cent of people take birth and die in the same bandwidth. Throughout their lives, they never try to change any aspect of their lives. They forget about their contribution to the world. People who are capable of understanding that their contribution can not only change their own lives but can also make a significant impact in changing the world and making it a beautiful place—these are the people who most of the world cannot understand. When these people speak, at first people laugh, then ignore them. Finally, they stay away and think of them as visionaries on a special mission.

Your body has seven energy points, called chakras, to manage seven different types of energy. Each of them has a particular bandwidth of upper frequency and lower frequency to absorb energy. But as these chakras keep on accumulating energies, not only does the pattern of these energy points suffer, but over a period of time we start attracting the wrong energy.

All we have to do to attract the energy of the universe is to channel it through these seven energy points. The beauty of these coiled energy chakras is that each one vibrates at a different frequency and each one of them is important. All of them are capable of accepting the energy level you are tuned to. For instance, in case your relationship chakra is imbalanced, then you will only attract people who are already messed up in their relationships. All the gurus will tell you how to attract people, but no one will tell you how you can attract the right people when you don't radiate the right energy. It is like you want to watch a crime series but your frequency is that of the Cartoon Network and no matter how much you try, you are not going to see crime series on that channel.

So, let us go through some rituals which will help you to attract the right energies in life.

## Understanding Energy Components

To make ourselves powerful, we will go through various rituals to gather energy, but first of all, we need to know the components and sources of energy, as increasing energy is a two-step process. The first step is: stop draining energy in useless acts. Second: continuously gain energy via the universe.

Now let us look at various energy components and break them down so it will be easier to identify what are the different energy sources, and which energy source we are lacking.

We as human beings are made of five elements. There is always some amount of imbalance in these elements. It is okay to have an imbalance in these elements, as the balanced being can only be God. Remember, when you are born as a human you will have all the good and bad qualities of a human. What the imbalance does is that you will have certain elements which will give you power while certain elements will drain you, and some elements will be neutral towards you. However, it is you who has to identify your power source.

The five elements present in our body are:

1. Water
2. Earth
3. Air
4. Fire
5. Ether or Sky

These are the five elements that make up our body, and these are the five energy sources which we require to grow in life. Each energy source has its specific function. When these five elements are imbalanced in us, we not only go through physical discomforts and diseases but also deficiency of so many other important things in life, such as the absence of love, money, growth and happiness.

## Air Element

Everything in life starts from a simple thought, a simple idea which can change everything around you. The quality of your thoughts will not only determine the quality of life you are living at present but also the life you are going to live in the future.

It is always one simple thought which can bring about a revolution in the world. It is therefore very important to keep our thought process in control at all times. Let us understand how thoughts are generated in our heads, and how controlling the thinking pattern can change the way you are living your life.

Our thoughts are generated by the atmosphere around us, the kind of people we are dealing with and the inputs that we gather in the form of media from TV, the Internet and other sources. Based on these inputs, our brain will start developing thoughts.

The Air element is your intellectual capability, your desires and aspirations, your ability to absorb knowledge and create a new world out of it, and your manipulative ability to change thoughts by interaction.

The seed of all problems lies in the Air element, as it is always one thought which, once it comes to your head can become a reality, as for anything in life to happen—good or bad—first a seed has to be sown in the brain and when the brain keeps getting inputs to water that seed, you will find ways to convert that thought into reality. That is why it is very important to discard anyone who is feeding you with negative thoughts.

\* \* \*

How and why do people become geniuses? Why do only a few become geniuses? I have analysed the charts of great minds. I looked for various combinations and, over a period of time, I found one thing the birth charts had in common: Their charts had an imbalanced energy.

Let us go through a simple ritual to control thoughts; when done continuously, this is a ritual that can give you insights into the universe.

Deep inside your brain, there lies a Pandora's box which can give you genius ideas which you have not even imagined. But to access this box and talk directly

27

to the universe, you need to first cut off the external factors which are actually draining your thinking capability by giving you unnecessary information. For example, have you noticed how people feel dizzy and sleep during a train or bus ride? The reason is when we look outside the window, the amount of information which is going into the brain is continuously increasing, which results in deep sleep.

A person who is a deep thinker will be a deep sleeper, as his brain is tired by the amount of information that has to be processed. When you go through your phone continuously, looking at various social media apps, you are providing information to the brain that is absolute garbage and will not result in any kind of personal or mental growth. Your Air element is getting disturbed and the ideas which were somewhere in your brain related to your personal growth are way down on the priority list.

Your brain has a rhythm of processing a particular thought and then responding to it. It leads from one thought to another and then one after another, it will keep on going to deeper levels of thinking. Imagine a room with a door followed by the same pattern— another room and another door. Each door has a different latch system, some take three seconds to open, while some doors can take up to fifteen seconds to open. Finally, after opening the door to the last room, you reach a treasure chest of brilliant ideas.

Some people take around ten minutes to reach this box of ideas, while some people will never even try to reach this box, as their thoughts are continuously disturbed by either phone notifications or other distractions. The rhythm of the brain is continuously disturbed, and they are never able to reach the deepest part of their brain where all intelligence and brilliant ideas lie. This is the reason why some people are confused and always complain that they have no clue about their life. All their decisions are taken subconsciously, as they do not have a deep understanding of the actions they are taking in life.

If you can remove distractions in life and continuously feed your brain via positive thoughts, whether it is by listening to meaningful songs or placing a beautiful picture of smiling kids on your desk, it will empower your thought process continuously, rather than watching TV or random videos on your phone.

Once you are alone and focusing on your work, then your brain starts forming a rhythm, so you can do something that will become a masterpiece in itself, as it would be the result of brilliant ideas generated from the deepest part of the brain. All solutions lie within you. All we need to do is sit down and meditate on a problem, think from a fresh mind and make a decision. The best time to make an important decision in life is early morning, around 5 a.m. This is the time when the energy in the sky will support you.

If, during your morning walk or while watering plants, you go through physical discomfort, it is your body showing you that you are not aligned with the universe, and there is an element that is not balanced inside you. The problem starts with a simple thought. The same discomfort that a person never wants to share with anyone creates a small blockage in the head related to that particular emotion. When you keep on creating various such blockages in your head, your actions will also be affected, and you will not be able to perform at your peak level because now you have created a boundary for yourself.

Imagine a dress which you loved a lot; the fabric, colour and comfort, everything was perfect and as you wish, but the moment someone pointed out something faulty about the dress, such as you are not looking good in it, you became conscious about the way you look, despite everything being great till that moment. Your brain has created a negative exclamation mark against that dress in your head, and next time, when you pick up this dress, this blockage will be there and you will skip wearing it and go for another one.

If your brain is so sensitive to one comment, then imagine how many great ideas and opportunities you might have rejected just because your brain was programmed earlier by negative influences.

The best way to remove these kinds of blockages is via rituals of self-affirmations and knowledge. Here is a step-by-step guide.

1) **Start with deep thinking habits and reducing any unwanted information.** Reduce your phone and TV time. In today's world, everyone is busy pushing their agenda; no one is on your side. Focus on information which will increase your knowledge and happiness, such as shows about ancient sciences, or a science documentary packed with facts. That would be a million times more useful than watching biased anchors in newsrooms, who are busy pushing agendas of a particular ideology.

    It was same thing that happened in Nazi Germany, and if you think you are not living in that kind of world, then you should watch a documentary on both world wars carefully and compare the situations.

2) **Read every day.** Every day, make it a ritual to read at least twenty pages of a book that is not related to your profession but to your life, such as something

on religion, self-help, fiction, biographies or—my favourite—stories about magic, as people who do not learn new things will easily feel depressed in life. Learning keeps the brain working and gives you new thoughts, which in turn makes you feel more confident.

3) **Pray.** Prayers are the most effective way to ask for answers. When you are praying to someone in the sky or someone who is deep-seated within you, you will be able to identify problems and the answers.

Let us come to a ritual of cleansing a deep-rooted thought. Whenever you feel stuck in life by your own thoughts, when you feel there is a mental blockage in starting a new phase of life and your brain is continuously going over and over the same problem again, then do these Vayu (Air) rituals.

1) **Conversations with God.** Imagine you are directly talking with God, and you have to address this problem to him. When you stand in front of a person who is running the whole universe, then you cannot start the conversation with complaints. Start with a small prayer of gratitude such as, 'I am thankful that today I am able to get out of my bed, and you have given me a chance to pray. I am thankful for my children, spouse, a home to live

in.' Give thanks for every single thing that you have taken for granted till now, and then in the end you can talk about your troubles.

I am sure by the time you will come to explain your trouble, you will not be able to even mention it and what you might be going through, as you yourself will know by this time how much the universe has given you on this earth.

Repeat this for several days, and daily, while doing this prayer, keep a fruit, flower or something to offer in love to the universe, and say, 'I am thankful that I can pray today.' Slowly you will see the negative blockages will start going away and new people will start coming into your life with new thoughts and energy.

2) **Changing the Air element.** Every place has a different amount of energy in the air. It depends on various geographical factors. When you breathe in the air in a new place, your thoughts change. Going to different parts of the country to meet new people and get new thoughts is extremely important for people who want to break the cycle of saturation; that is why taking a vacation and going to the beach or mountains is important at least once a year, so that you can enjoy the breeze and new air can circulate new thoughts inside you.

3) **Chanting mantras.** Mantras consist of universal sounds, and these hymns and rhythms create an effect in the brain which eventually changes the thinking pattern by attracting the energies to pacify negative thoughts.

Each mantra has a deity, and each deity is associated with a particular task, so when a mantra is chanted every day at a specific time in a specific place, what we are doing is attracting energy from the sky which we are lacking in our thought process.

One basic sound of the universe is the humming sound of 'Om'. 'Om' is a general mantra and contains a lot of possibilities, but it is a good point to start cleansing yourself as, when we continuously repeat 'Om', suddenly the brain starts going into a reset mode. When we recite this mantra with controlled breath throughout the day, you cleanse the Air element of the body.

When you chant any *stotra* that is of a short duration, such as the Hanuman Chalisa or Kaal Bhairav, do it at least eleven times. You need to become a part of Hanumanji, and to do that takes time. You will get the energy via the universe, and in a few days, you will see the change in your voice, your facial features along with other behavioural changes. These changes happen as your body is taking in the new energy.

## Fire Element

The Fire element is about challenges: your ability to move ahead in life and the sacrifices you are ready to make, how easily you are able to adapt to a new situation, and your courage and leadership skills at times of adversity.

When the Fire element is imbalanced in a body, the person is unable to take new initiatives as they are always busy doing tasks. They keep on running from one place to another without applying much thought to it; all their efforts end up being in vain.

A person whose Fire element is not balanced will not take some time off to think, 'What are my priorities? What will be the result of the work I am doing, in the long run?' This person is unable to have a long-term vision in life and will realize too late in their life that they have wasted their time doing things that had no meaning at all, as taking new initiatives is not this person's cup of tea.

Fire represents new beginnings, and when people lack the courage to start new things, it is because they are too afraid to take a risk; they become so comfortable in their misery that any new idea scares them.

Fire marks new beginnings. In almost all cultures, fire rituals hold the same significance—to leave behind the negative and start a new journey by lighting a fire. Rituals of fire show us new paths and give a sign to the universe that now we are ready for a new beginning in life.

On a full moon night, lighting a lamp outside the house, on the roof or balcony, is a way to attract energies which can help you grow in life. If we can calibrate things in this ritual, magic is created, or some people call it *tantra*. The more synchronized you become with the universe, you will understand why this was not taught to you in school, and why this was kept hidden. And this is true: these rituals were limited to royal palaces only, as it was the king who would require these rituals to live a long healthy life and attract prosperity, and if the king was happy, the kingdom would prosper.

So how to calibrate this ritual? Based on your problem, you can choose your day and direction to perform this remedy and then do it once a week on a specific day.

| Weekday | Problem | Direction |
|---------|---------|-----------|
| Monday | Emotional support and happiness | North-East |
| Tuesday | Health and courage | South |
| Wednesday | Business relationships and management | North-West |

| Weekday | Problem | Direction |
|---------|---------|-----------|
| Thursday | Kids and peace | North |
| Friday | Marriage and money | North-West |
| Saturday | Health and work | West |
| Sunday | Vision and fame | East |

So let us say you are facing problems in your marriage. Check which particular month has a dark night falling on a Friday and, starting from that Friday, for fourteen weeks regularly light a lamp in the north-west direction on your house roof or balcony.

This is because on this night a lot of positive energies will enter your house. You will be able to see the difference in two to three weeks of lighting a lamp.

## Water Element

This is the element which makes us human. Since the human body is 70 per cent water, you can say 70 per cent of our problems arise from this content, as water has the ability to store memories and, based on what we are continuously accumulating in our body, our perception towards the outer world is built.

When the Water element is balanced, a person is able to continuously chuck out negative thoughts and feelings and is able to see the brighter side in any situation, without getting stuck and hampering their emotional growth.

We are capable of loving someone or hating someone as we store emotions about incidents in our bodies. To love anyone else in this world, a person should be confident enough to love themselves. People stop loving themselves due to guilt or fear as the world wants you to live in guilt—guilt is the most effective way to sell religion, ideology and even products through body shaming. For example, in a country like India, beauty products to change the skin tone is a big business. This could only be possible by creating a feeling of guilt/shame about being dark in people's minds through advertising.

We feel hurt when people don't treat us as we want them to treat us. This is emotional dependency, as your emotional brain expects certain types of behaviour from other people and, on rejection, it retaliates in various forms. When you stop your emotional dependence on other people, and your mood, actions and life are not at the mercy of other people's reactions, this is true emotional independence.

This is one of those valuable lessons of life that I learnt after India's loss in the Cricket World Cup in 2003. That was the last time I watched a cricket match as well. So, as a seventeen-year-old, I was extremely excited about the Indian team playing in the World Cup. But anyone who watched that match knows that India not only lost that final but that the performance of the Indian team was at the mercy of the Australian cricket team. The Indian team played that match like a headless chicken, with no clue about what to do.

The impact of this loss was so deep on my mental health that I couldn't sleep for several nights. I was going through emotional pain, and I was not able to express it to anyone. It was the same thing that millions of fans experienced at the end of the *Games of Thrones* show because they felt it did not end in a proper manner. When we watch a movie, we expect it to end in a particular manner, and if it does not happen, our brain is not able to make sense of the conclusion.

In all these examples, it was our emotional body that was so attached to these characters that we couldn't accept that things could happen against our wishes.

When you start your journey of emotional independence, you experience a sense of liberation that you have not felt before. When you begin, you might be scared, as your brain has not experienced this kind of emotional independence till now.

If I ask you, how much you trust your spouse, you will say 100 per cent. But if I say to you, 'Imagine your spouse is cheating on you.' You might feel a bit uncomfortable, and to make you extremely uncomfortable, I tell you that your spouse is cheating on you with your best friend. You will be devastated, as now your brain has started developing negative feelings, as you expect your spouse to be loyal towards you.

Your emotional brain wants to control everyone, and any deviation from it is not acceptable to you. It doesn't matter whether your spouse has an affair with someone or not, as the person who is not loyal will never be loyal under any condition. You can spy on them 24/7, and still, the person will find a way to cheat. On the other hand, a loyal person will remain loyal irrespective of whether you are watching them or not.

So, what is emotional independence and how to achieve it?

It takes time to walk on this path, but once you get into the habit of gaining emotional independence, trust me, you will be invincible on this earth as you have gained control over 70 per cent of your body and 70 per cent of your life is not clean as a highway.

Start with the simple exercise of repeating this mantra several times a day. 'Aham Brahmasmi'— which means, I am God, everything is inside me. You can make your own mantra in your mother tongue as well, such as something that means 'I am alone'. When you start realizing that, in this life, you came alone and you have to go alone and the rest all are only your co-passengers in the same compartment, that a few people will live with you for some days, months or years, and then everyone has their own journey, you will stop having expectations from anyone.

When expectation ends, suddenly the person becomes blunt and truthful with everyone, as there is no fear of anyone leaving them. When I started this experiment, instead of people going away from my life, I had better and more honest conversations with people, which was not possible earlier.

Secondly, stop listening to information and news about someone else from a third person. I have made it a rule not to listen to any stories about relatives, friends or even competitors from anyone else. Whenever someone starts complaining about a person or starts a sentence with 'Don't tell this to anyone . . .', at that very moment, I say, 'If you are going to tell me anything, I will call that person and clarify it.'

Slowly people who were wasting my time with useless talk stopped calling me, and it brought immense peace to my life. The bottom line is, do not get involved in conversations which are not useful at all.

What you are doing by following these practices is that you are controlling the garbage which can affect your emotional health.

Only in your head is there a need to control everyone you think is associated with you. When emotional independence comes, not only will you find yourself relaxed and happy, but you'll also see that people will want to be a part of your life, as no one in this world wants to associate themselves with a person who is fearful, emotionally imbalanced and unhappy.

It will start with your spouse, co-workers, employees. You need to start trusting them, and instead of focusing on them, you should now focus on yourself and the roles you play in life, such as boss, employee, guru, student, spouse. Ask yourself whether you are honest in every role or not.

Am I working with honesty at my workplace?

A person who is not honest with themself will never be happy in life, as their emotional diet will be compensated by some other flaw or frustration and by blaming others. We are living in a society where a lot of religious hate is propagated and we know this is intentionally done, so next time, when you write on your social media about any other religion, ask yourself, 'Am I following my religion in a good enough manner?'

People who don't follow their own religion are the ones busy finding faults in other people's practices. You become honest with your religion, and no one will ever be able to harm your religion.

For people who do not have control over their emotions, their emotional instability makes their lives miserable, as any external thought makes them miserable at any point in time.

A person who has the Water element imbalanced in their body will make erratic decisions and will be a source of trouble for everyone around them, as this person's mood, behaviour and actions are not synchronized. When these people make mistakes, they try to compensate and end up making some other kind of mistake.

The Water element is emotion, healing, feeding, compassion and doing good for everyone you come in contact with. The Water element is what governs your ability to touch people's lives.

When you become a balanced person, suddenly you will see you are a blessing for society, as now you can show the path to several other souls in life. When you start this chain of healing and fixing internal feelings, people will feel blessed just by coming in contact with you.

## Earth Element

The Earth element is practical implementation on the ground, the calculative ability of the brain, dealing with day-to-day practical problems, managing people for success, fully executing tasks and being helpful to society.

The Earth element helps you make practical decisions and make the best possible use of resources around you. When the Earth element is very strong, the person is very methodical and can work with different details to execute any plan. When the same element is disturbed, then the person might have some of the best plans in the world, but using this knowledge is practically impossible for them.

Anything which you can feel or has materialistic value falls under the domain of the earth, and from this, you can understand the value of this component. If a person is resourceful, then it is only because the Earth element in the body is responding well. A person with extreme imbalance of the Earth element suffers from a lack of money.

Start balancing the Earth element by controlling your food habits. Food has a great amount of energy from the earth, as all crops and vegetables are grown on land and, depending on the type of food consumed, our Earth element increases or decreases. I have discussed this component in detail in a later part.

## Ether Element

The Ether element is your long-term planning, satisfaction and contentment, your ability to experience bliss in life. In those moments of bliss, you feel the middle part of your chest is opening and you have so much love and gratitude towards the universe that you want everyone to experience this. Every morning, I wake up with the feeling of so much gratitude and happiness that it feels like a dream come true; this is only due to an abundance of energy.

The Ether element is not visible but is the most important element in nature, as, without a sense of peace and happiness, no person on earth can enjoy themselves. Imagine a life where you have every other element, but you don't have peace of mind. This is provided by the Ether element, and it comes from devotion, prayers and helping other people.

On YouTube and Facebook, there are several thousand videos of people helping a homeless person or beggars, and millions of viewers love watching these videos. Any specific reason? The reason is that our souls want to help the world, we want to see happiness on another human's face. It gives us a feeling of contentment and pride that we are able to bring light to someone's life.

\* \* \*

Problems in life will never end until and unless you raise your energy levels so that nothing affects you—like flowers being thrown on an iron statue. This is a continuous process, to gather energy from different elements. You need to choose your path from one of the elements of Nature—Agni, Prithvi, Vayu, Jal, Akash. All remedies prescribed in the classics, such as *havan*, chanting, stones, visiting temples and taking a bath in rivers, are based on these five elements.

When you practise these rituals, you will not be able to lead a normal lifestyle, as you will now have raised your energy levels. Your desire to meet people goes down, and you have to try to act normal among people. But still, your energy cannot lie low, that is why animals and other energies will keep following you. You will keep on getting messages from the universe about things which are about to happen.

When people perform havan regularly, their Agni element goes to a different level. They will propose new theories and ways to do things. This is what the energy of invoking Agni does. Their *agya* chakra and *pitt* content are so high that, any time they do a havan, the energy will manifest itself. While doing a havan, when you sit in front of the fire and offer things to Agni with devotion, you will get the sense that something has changed, as the fire *tattva* inside you has received energy from Agni.

People who dip in water regularly and continuously work on their emotional brain can heal anyone with words and heal the community by collective efforts.

When you do sadhana over a long period, you don't realize how mad you have become until you meet normal people. From the way you dress to the way you think, it makes you feel these people need enlightenment and you wonder why they can't see this.

So, choose a path of energy to sort out your issues in life and keep on doing these rituals to get energy from the five elements.

# 4

# Energy Devices of the Universe—Yantra

*Yantra* is a Sanskrit word for machine. In this universe, to convert one energy form to another form, you need a machine, in the same way that you require a device to communicate with your friends and family on the phone. As technology progresses, every day a new feature is added to the device. Similarly, to communicate with different realms and the universe, we need yantras to carry our messages. Yantras connect us to different realms so we can receive messages and power.

Yantras are geometrical patterns which, when combined with a particular sound, space and time, give results. Humans call it God. As humans, we have a tendency wherein when we do not want to understand or face something, or if we experience any inexplicable phenomena, we call it God.

In this book, we will start with two very simple patterns and yantras to help you attract energy. The effects of these yantras are powerful and these will help you experience the magic of the universe. The beauty of the energy principle is that, as long as you follow the steps, you will get the results.

Today's technology is still emerging and there are instances when, despite all the development, science will say that they are not able to connect you with the universe. I have some very simple rituals for this, derived from Hinduism. However, instead of following them for the sake of it, try and understand the science behind them; this way, you can connect yourself to a higher energy source.

As this is the first time I am writing on this topic, I will let my readers experience and work with simple energies without using any complex terms and names so that even a lay person can understand the process. Many of my astrology students will be able to relate it to planets and nakshatra energies. But in this book, I have not used any astrological terms, as I want people to heal themselves without having to go through astrological knowledge and patterns.

## Signs of the Universe—Pathways

In the same way that you require a signboard on a motorway to reach a particular location, or Google Maps these days, similarly, the universe has its sign language to transfer a particular energy to a particular person.

The universe requires markings to identify people for certain causes, and this is why appearance is the first way to change energy.

When you are walking on a road, even if you don't realize it, your brain is creating markings; to remember any route, your brain creates anchors so you can remember the way. For instance, if you are walking on a road, the moment you see a big yellow M on top of a building, your brain stores it as a McDonald's restaurant. Your brain has all the information related to the menu, taste, service of the restaurant, etc. You know what to expect when you walk into that establishment, and it is now a reference point. Similarly, some people are hidden in plain sight, and a few will make an impression, such as a person walking in maroon robes with a shaved head. You know that the person is a Tibetan monk.

When your brain looks at a person with special markings, such as robes, shoes, tattoos, piercings or any special body feature, that person gets attention. Similarly, when you start using certain symbols, you will get the attention of the universe. The universe also looks for signs to identify its people, and it does so by your actions. I am listing a few markings below. You should try all of them and see the results as an experiment. We tried this with a group of people on Facebook. The results were extraordinary. Some of them are mentioned at the end of the chapter with symbols. The same markings are called 'yantras' in Hinduism, 'signs' in the West and '*nishan*' in Persian. But all of them have the same purpose and act as a symbol for energies.

Understand yantra first. As I mentioned earlier, a yantra means an instrument or machinery which is made to perform certain tasks. But unlike any electrical or mechanical machine, this is a spiritual machine. It is a pattern or a drawing to attract certain energies, just like we receive radio signals using electronic components. Similarly, to attract a specific energy from the universe, we use certain patterns and shapes.

The most common and easy cosmic pattern you will see everywhere is a triangle, which is used to channelize energy from space to earth. Triangles are the gateway to exit or enter the world and are used as a communication device. Any yantra which is built with the help of triangles represents that we are channelling power from one world to another. Even in the human body, genitals form triangles, so as to transfer energy from one medium to another. This is also the shape of the universe.

In ancient times, structures were made at specific locations and with a particular design. One of the common structures you will find all across the globe are pyramids. Pyramids have been made all around the world and are engineering marvels. Have you ever thought why these pyramids were built all across the globe: in Egypt, China, Japan and even in India? All have similar structures, where the upper portion is extremely narrow and forms the shape of a triangle. These structures were created to channel energy from space and make these buildings storehouses of cosmic energy. Even the locations were carefully chosen for these buildings. I have discussed this on my YouTube channel Lunar Astro as well.

There are different ways you can build these yantras or machines to get a burst of energy in a particular form to perform a desired task. I am more focused on getting you introduced to the energy of the universe. I will begin with the triangle pattern.

## Upward Triangle

If you draw a triangle pointing upwards on a piece of paper, like in the figure given above, and place it on your front gate, or if you get a tattoo of a triangle on your body, you have given a message to the universe that you are ready to receive energy from space. Now, through this particular symbol, you will start receiving energies to get upliftment in life. Upward Triangles are good for spiritual growth and when you have to learn subjects about which there is no literature available.

Whenever you draw an Upward Triangle and want to connect to the universe, it is necessary to place the picture of the triangle near a window. Preferably, it should be placed under the open sky where this triangle can receive energy without obstructions. But as the human body is a conductor and offers a path of least resistance, any symbol will work better on the human body rather than on a piece of paper. So, you can create this as a locket in a metal such as copper, silver or gold, which are good conductors of energy. The effects will be amplified due to the easy pathway.

If you get a 3D model of a pyramid made from a conducting material, then the effects are much more pronounced. The top portions of all the ancient Hindu temples were made in either copper or gold. Similarly, ancient churches have either a gold cross or a roof painted with a coat of gold. The reason why these places have energy-conducting materials on top is so that when the universe sees the marking, it starts sending energy down. Energy follows the path of least resistance.

When someone visits these places, the person experiences a rise in energy levels and sees magical changes happening in their lives. Life starts changing as you are now in a structure which is continuously absorbing energy from the sky. The moment you enter this structure, which is built for prayer, there is a sudden increase of energy in the body.

People say that they experience miracles in their lives, and that, they have had the experience of meeting God. They at times feel a sudden moment of bliss, like the world has stopped moving and they have got into a zone which seems like they are in another world. The whole world feels nothing more than a virtual reality, where everyone is running around without knowing the true meaning of energy and life. In that zone, you feel that the power of the universe is so big that all your problems just leave your mind, your soul wants to rise high and there are butterflies in your stomach. This is nothing other than the person's energy levels increasing by visiting such places. Imagine what will be your state when I ask you to continuously absorb energy into your body.

WhatsApp Message on 12 March 2022 from a US citizen:

[8:49 PM, 3/12/2022]: Dear Sir, With the triangle kept on my desk, a very heavy decoration mirror cracked outside our bedroom and the very next day my land deal that was on hold for a month went through.

The message below was from Pawan Pauriyal, on the Lunar Astro Facebook page:

Remedies Result.

I made this yantra with a colour pen the day Deepanshu Giri Sir posted this.

Result.

Day 1 - The money I had invested through my friend, 20% I got back. Even though all his investments are stuck he returned me some amount.

Day 2 - The paper was missing from my table. Realized this on the 3rd day.

Day 3 - Made the yantra again on paper.

Day 4 - 60% money I got back. Only 20% remaining.

I returned that to my sister as I had taken that money from her. I thought once I get enough profit, I can buy predictive astrology course from Lunar Astro. Back in Nov 2021 I have completed BA. And now I am committing myself to astrology. Om Namah Shivaya.

Thank you so much Deepanshu Sir for your guidance. You are our guardian superhuman. Spreading such ray of hope that we start believing in ourselves more and more. God will bless you with abundance. God will bless you with more power and more positivity so that you will make the world a better place to live in. Thank you very very much. Thank you Sir. God bless you. Thanks a ton.

What do you think happened in both these cases? Why did something suddenly surge in their lives? These people attracted energy and experienced the results by connecting themselves to the energy source.

At the same time, it is important for people who want to excel in the field of spirituality and energy to cover their heads all the time. It does not matter which religious place you are trying to enter, you will always find that covering the head is a part of the ritual from the olden days. When people were more careful about energy balances, every man and woman would cover their heads all the time. Even now, spiritual people always cover their heads. This is because the top of your head is one of the important energy points. It is also known as the crown chakra.

Rabbi, priest, panditji, maulana, pathji—all of them belong to different religions and are from different parts of the world, but all of them usually cover their heads with different types of caps. The reason being that these people have to protect themselves from excessive energy going through their heads as it might create an imbalance.

Whenever you enter any temple or perform any ritual of Hinduism, one is always asked to cover the head, as energy should not directly hit the top portion of the head. In the olden days, it was women who were not exposed to many energies and were more sensitive to energies than men. This is why women were always advised to cover their heads. When the head is covered there is protection from the direct strike of energy. The head radiates energy all the time and this energy will be wasted if the head is not covered.

As mentioned earlier, the Upward Triangle is for spiritual growth. Downward Triangles are good for material growth—i.e., when you have to excel in things which already exist in earthly planes. A Downward Triangle sucks in energy from the earth, as the earth is another source which is looking to deliver energy. The earth has so much potential and energy that has been stored over long a period of time. The moment you have given an indication to the universe that you are open to absorbing energy from the earth, you will start receiving that energy. If you are using the Downward Triangle, the best way to get energy from the earth is by walking barefoot on grass.

Let me give you a practical example. Johnny Depp became an actor in the 1980s; he started his career with minor roles and a TV show. In 1993, which was the year he signed on three big movies, he got a tattoo of a Downward Triangle on his body. This was the year when there was a big leap for the actor in Hollywood, as he started getting noticed in the industry.

Downward Triangles attract wealth, but these triangles also bring a lot of addiction and morality issues, as Downward Triangles channel the earthy energy in the form of materialism. Energy from space is lighter and gives a feeling of bliss and contentment. Energy from space will give you things where you can experience bliss. It is similar to what you feel when you visit any temple; what you get in return has no monetary value but only you know what you have felt. On the other hand, energy from earth is full of earthy desires and it always comes with other problems. If you do not control this energy, it will lead to destruction. Earthy energy has a monetary value; when anything is earthy you can smell it, feel it, taste it and it has a value attached to it.

You can do this as an experiment. Place the shape of an upward or downward triangle outside your house and you will see the number of unwanted visitors increase. What you have done is that you have given a mark to the universe that you are open to receiving energy. A warning: Please don't place the image of a triangle on your phone by changing the wallpaper to a triangle or triangular pattern. When we posted about the experiment on the Facebook group of Lunar Astro, by evening many people complained that their phones had either stopped working or hung multiple times. They had placed a triangle as a wallpaper and as the phone has a battery connected to it, this amplifies the energy of the pattern several hundred times. You will suddenly experience a lot of activity happening on your phone as what you have done is you have opened a gateway—a yantra—a passage for energy. So just by drawing the pattern, you will be giving a signal to the universe that you are open to receiving energy either in physical form or spiritual form.

Some of the people who made a mark on their main gate with colour, experienced fluctuations in electricity, with electrical items suddenly breaking down. A few people reported that the number of unwanted people visiting their house had increased on that day. One person reported that he received a package from Amazon and the contents of the parcel were more expensive than what was ordered.

This is what universal markings do in life.

This is the simplest way to attract energy. You can have more complex patterns to attract very specific energy in your life by making similar patterns on your laptop or phone. Depending on how precisely you make this yantra, the clearer will be the energy you attract in life. So, while drawing it as a tattoo or wearing it as a pendant, make sure each side of the triangle is equal, with no wear and tear on either side.

In the next chapter, we will look into more advanced forms of yantra. But do not trust that it works until and unless you yourself experience the energy. Like every machine, there is an input and an output. We need to check whether the mark we have given to the universe is working or not. This is the way we are going to do this.

The best way to balance the energy of the sky and the energy of the earth is to make the pattern of a star with the help of two triangles. This particular combination is used to attract energy which is balanced in nature. A star is capable of creating a wonderful balance of both energies.

On the other hand, if you make repetitive patterns, such as a concentric double upward triangle or a downward triangle, you multiply the energy, and this energy comes with obsessive behaviour. Concentric triangles in one direction only should not be used until and unless advised by an experienced person, as it can create havoc in life.

We will leave the yantra part here to let you work with the energy of yantras. As an exercise, draw one of the yantras, either an upward triangle or a downward triangle or a star. You should experience the energy realm yourself and see what happens when you give a mark to the universe. As, until and unless you experience it, you will never be convinced of the power of this book or the upcoming techniques.

## How to Check if the Yantra Is Working

When you buy a new phone, you probably have a good idea about how it will work as you are familiar with phones. But what about energy patterns? I am asking you to draw triangles and later on other specific shapes. How are you going to be sure that these energy symbols are working or not? I want you to ask these logical questions when you do something with faith, as

this whole world works on the principle of energy. You should be able to see this magic at any point of time in your life. If you cannot feel the energy of the universe, then it is not worth reading this book or doing any of the rituals.

When you start receiving energy via patterns, the first thing that will happen within a span of one to three days is that you will suddenly experience that some of your electrical equipment is not working, some mirror or crockery may suddenly break, or the water pipe will burst. Sometimes you will also see this happening in your neighbourhood. This is a result of negative energy leaving you, which was stored inside these places.

If this does not happen in the first three days, then try placing the yantra in a much more effective direction.

If you are wearing it as a pendant, you will not be able to sleep properly. Due to extra energy, your mind will go into an active state all the time. So even when you try to sleep, your brain will still be in an active state. For the first few days, test the yantra pendant. Try sleeping while wearing it. As it gets more and more power from the universe, you will see your brain becoming more active in the day. At night, you will have to remove this pendant to sleep properly.

With patterns, we will experience a very clear connection with our inner world. The moment we think about something, within a few hours we start getting signals. News of someone comes with an opportunity from the same direction. The reason it has happened is because we project that thought out into the universe very strongly via this pattern.

You can also place this yantra on any person who is addicted or going through problems which they don't want to discuss, and you will still see results.

# 5

# The Sound of the Universe—Mantras

Yantras are combined with mantras or sounds to communicate with the universe. Imagine you are driving your car, enjoying your ride, but suddenly you hear a police siren. Without thinking for a second, your subconscious brain will tell you what to do next as the sound of a siren is marking in your brain the urgency of the situation and telling you to respond accordingly. Every word you speak has a picture attached to it, such as, when I say 'hospital', your brain will automatically pull up a picture of a hospital—that is why humans respond to language, pitch tone and words instantly.

Similarly, the universe has its own system, and it responds on a particular frequency. Perhaps certain energies are attracted towards certain rhythms and patterns, like in an office building, when there is a siren, everyone gathers on their muster station. Similarly, certain sounds are generated to gather energy from space.

When you add sound to any yantra, then it is for a specific purpose. Like when you write OM, it represents infinite possibilities to get connected to the universe and give you spiritual upliftment. When you add certain sounds, called seed mantras, which are based on these mantras, other mantras are created. These mantras act as seeds for other mantras and are very powerful when mixed with yantras. Begin with 'Om', as before we go into more intense energies, you should have a body to absorb it. It is better to get used to subtle energy first.

When mantras or sounds are expressed in a rhythm, they create a pattern and this process is called cymatics, which means that every sound has a shape, and this shape is manifested in the form of yantras as well. When we listen to music, our brain creates a pattern in our head, which in turn makes us travel in different zones altogether. You must have experienced it while listening to your favourite song, which makes you go into a different world. Music lets your logical brain shut down and takes you into a state of bliss for a moment. You can never explain the feeling of listening to certain words of a song. When the words, rhythm and feeling of music are in resonance with your body, magic happens.

Indian classical music is made to address seven energy points in your body. That is why ragas are divided according to specific times of the day that they should be played. Music can not only heal you but can also let you get connected to different worlds by making a yantra pattern in your brain and attracting energies from different worlds. Especially before sleeping, when we listen to these soul ragas, our soul travels and gets connected to various energy sources. For connection, we use yantras, mudras and various patterns.

Sometimes, when we wake up in the morning, we have a good or bad hair day. We may wonder what makes our hair super cool one day and really bad on another day when we are using the same shampoo and following the same process every time. The answer is the energy in your head. People with excessive energy in their heads always have their hair standing up; their hair never settles in the middle portion where there is a place for a ponytail. This is because every night you absorb energy from space while you are asleep and in your dreams. Your dreams are a part of the energy you are receiving. That is why it is strictly recommended to not keep any electronic item or utensil next to your head. One way to absorb negative energy is to keep a glass of water next to your head to give you a healing effect while you are asleep.

The patterns that are formed while we sleep make us feel either energetic or lethargic the next morning. The pattern formation depends on what our energy source was that night, whether we drained or gained energy. Tell me what will happen when you sleep and your head has a messy pattern—you will attract messy energy. When you sleep with a yantra pattern in your head, you attract that energy in the night.

The seven *svara* represent the seven planets in Jyotish, starting from *shadja*. I always recommend ragas as a form of therapy before sleeping. Music not only helps with good sleep but also makes a pattern in your brain like cymatics, and these patterns are yantras of different energies in the sky. Raag Yaman, for instance, soothes you before sleep and gives a healing effect, as it forms a yantra of healing in your head. When you sleep, you will start attracting all the energies which can heal you and take pain away from your life. This is a process to know yourself and turn yourself towards yantra and travel to different worlds, to experience things of several lifetimes. It is possible that you may not get good dreams. But these dreams will show you why you are stuck in life and what you can do to move ahead in life.

Some people will see dead people asking for things such as food, clothes, water or an unfulfilled desire they might have. They may be complaining for a certain reason, so the moment you fulfil their desires, you will get tremendous results in your life. Let me give you some insight into this. When I was getting married, one of my maternal cousins was going through a medical procedure in her stomach. I used to visit her regularly, and in the same way, as all girls ask their brothers, she asked me what gift I would give her when I got married. I told her to get all right and I would buy her a saree equal to her weight once she was out of the hospital. Unfortunately, she was not able to make it through the surgery.

One night close to the day she died, after I listened to a raga, she appeared in my dream. I saw her dressed in a red lehnga, walking into a marriage venue. For most men, clothes don't matter. But for women, marriage outfits hold a special place. She walked up to me saying, 'Brother, my dress is still due.' This was around eight years after her death, and the moment I gave a similar red outfit to a girl who was getting married, I experienced a sudden rise in my life.

Dreams are the easiest way to get connected to a different universe because you will be connected to different energy sources. This energy is now attracted towards you, as now you have connected yourself via your body yantra to the universe. You spend thousands to achieve a state of trance. I am giving you that same opportunity in one night to fast-forward your journey. It is not about distance, it is about your energy and how fast you can travel.

If you are suffering in your profession and don't know what your mistake is or why you deserve to be in such a position, don't you ask this question every night before you sleep? Answers can only be given by the universe and for this you should get ready to travel every night to different worlds to see why you are going through a particular phase.

There are seven different realms which exist, other than the earth, and these are parallel universes. We think that the whole universe is as per our understanding of it, but we only live in a part of virtual reality. There are other realms where rules are different from this particular universe. Every realm has its own set of rules, like we have natural laws such as gravity, space and time. But when we start connecting to the supreme power, we can have access to unlimited power and abundance as we tend to understand this universe better.

You have already been to different realms in your previous births. You are born in this universe based on your actions in your past life. These seven different realms are further divided into two parts each, the upper universe and the lower universe, making it seven above the earth and seven below the earth.

Rastalak Lok is the universe of beauty and music. The whole purpose of living beings over there is to enjoy life through various activities, such as singing, dancing, creating various types of chemicals to stimulate the brain to experience bliss. But if in this life you are not happy and you have never got the feeling of extreme happiness without any material things, then you are suffering from crimes you have committed in this particular realm. You need to travel to this realm to see the cause and solution for this.

In your sleep, when you travel to a particular realm, you will get an idea of the solution as well. You will get to know the story which no astrologer can tell you. You will face your past life karma, as whatever question you ask the universe that night, with the yantra in your head, you will get connected to the same realm that night. Below, I have listed various ragas and the problems they can solve.

Once, a person was facing a government enquiry and was suspended from his job. I asked him to listen to a raag and note down his dream first thing in the morning. This person woke up with tears of grief and a very heavy heart. In his dream, he had seen a house and a family that he was a part of. One of the family members committed suicide after a fight with him over food. That relative went to his room and hanged himself, and the person was unable to save him. It was a very painful dream as it was so real that he could see the stool was blue and chipped in various places. When this person was trying to get the body down, even in the dream, he was apologizing for the fight and grieving for the family member.

This one incident shook the person so badly that, after this, his fights with his siblings stopped. This astral travel helped the person to understand his family members. The immense grief of losing a family member in the past was what he had carried with him. After six months he tried this again, and this time he saw two brothers starving for food outside a mud house, eating every single grain of rice that was on the floor. Again, this was very painful. But the brothers had a lot of love and affection for each other, and one was feeding the other. In the same dream, he saw that he got access to bags of rice but at the cost of his big brother becoming a slave at someone's house. He again woke up with not a very good feeling. All this that the person was experiencing was from his past life.

Both the dreams were about the person's brother, whom he had lost. This was the crime he had committed in his past life and was the reason why he was now experiencing problems related to his profession. In this life, when his siblings were asking for more money and a share in the property, it was only because of the debt in his past life. Once he let go of the dispute with his siblings, suddenly the professional enquiry he was facing was stopped.

If you want the remedy of a lifetime, work on your energy, as that is going to change everything around you. You attract what you radiate. This is the first step towards astral projection. You will see your past life as strange dreams that will come to you to remind you of various things, such as school friends and unknown people. In one or two days, the same people will come in front of you.

I have done this experiment several times and this works in real-time—it is so powerful. All the rituals which I am explaining in this book have been personally tried and tested by me as well as by people on Facebook. You can also follow the Facebook page of Lunar Astro to get involved in this in a better way.

As an experiment, I tried a particular raag which I believe attracts energy randomly. Whenever I start playing Raag Darbari while driving, suddenly people make a U-turn in front of a car, or some kind of accident happens. Whereas if I start playing Raag Madhumas, the trip is as smooth as it can be. By experimenting, I am very sure of the results that any raag will give, so you can plan your travel to different realms every night.

When you start performing this experiment, always keep a notepad on the side of the bed, and first thing in the morning write down as many details of the dream as you can. Then, try to relate it to your life and, next, try with another realm. Each time you will have different experiences.

One of my school friends tried this to get married, as he was thirty-two years old and had not been able to find anyone. I suggested that he try this dream travel. Every time he travelled, he saw a burning hut and different portions of the same story. But all of it seemed to belong in a place like China—and he had never visited that country. Every time he travelled in his dream, he got more information about the place. Something very strange happened during this period. Out of the blue, his boss told him he had to make a trip to China. This person had never been out of the country and was a CNC machine operator. Since they were importing this machine from China, they wanted a technician to travel along with the team to test it on the spot.

I told him that his travel to China was not an ordinary journey, as now strange things would happen, such as losing money, meeting special people, and so on. He had initiated this journey via travelling in his dreams, so he needed to be careful about fire. On his trip, my friend met a Chinese lady and married her a year later. This lady's grandparents had been killed in a house fire.

Can you join the dots now of dream travel and why this boy, who didn't know any other language except Hindi, had managed to travel to China and marry a woman from there at a later age? Once you start doing this experiment, it will go to a crazy level of manifestation in your life. You will feel that the real world is something else and what we are living in is just a virtual reality.

## List of Ragas and Problems They Can Solve

- Problems related to children, honour, getting a position in life, relationships with father and government—Raag Tanpura, Raag Shadbhinna, Raag Darbari
- Mental peace, relations with mother, happiness, calmness, family atmosphere, emotional trauma and pain—Raag Shudh, Raag Komal, Raag Yaman, Raag Hansdhawani

- Property-related issues, blood-related problems, violence and accidents—Bhairvai, Asavi, Thodi
- Education-related troubles, fights with siblings, thyroid and hormonal imbalance, communication, business, friends—Gandharva, Kalyan, Poorvi
- Relationship issues, money-related troubles—Nat Bhairav, Brindabani Sarang
- Lack of happiness, motivation, purpose, intangible happiness missing—Raag Shudha
- Profession-related issues, long-term diseases, chronic troubles—Jaunpuri, Kirwani, Neelambri

# 6

# Synchronicity of Time

When your actions are synchronized with the energy in the universe, you do not have to put in much effort with a particular task. The universe's energy is positive for specific tasks at specific times, so if you are in synchronicity with it, things flow easily.

For example, during the months of September and October, there is a surge in the download of health apps, gym membership subscriptions and other health-related activities. The energy of the universe is in the correction phase. By paying attention to health issues at this point of time, you will attract energy to heal yourself. Trying to quit any addiction or resolving court cases and litigation during this time will get you extraordinary results.

Similarly, 15 April to 15 May is an excellent period for conception, starting new learning, moving on and beginning a new life, as the energy of the universe is supporting you in this cause.

The universe has a pattern of synchronicity when energy levels in the atmosphere are vibrant and high, or very low. The energy levels being transmitted from the universe are for certain tasks. This is why it is important to be in synchrony with the universe. After so much research scientists have found out that if we do not resist our natural body clock to wake up and sleep, there is a natural happiness which generates in the body. Going against the body clock is one of the main causes of depression.

Similarly, when you go against the universal clock, life not only gets difficult, but you also feel as if the whole universe is working against you. The truth is that you are like a driver who is driving in the opposite direction on the highway and blaming everyone else for colliding with you. The moment you are in synchrony with the direction of the highway, all obstacles vanish.

There are also special days, seasons and months for specific tasks. The energy in the universe helps or resists tasks you want to perform. That is why, in Hinduism, for every special occasion, a person will visit a panditji and ask for a *mahurat*. Or, these days, people go to the website of Lunar Astro to ask about rituals to be performed on special occasions.

The best way to figure this out is to look for special days in your life, as this is your personal calendar for performing rituals. These special days can be your birthday, your marriage anniversary, the birthday of a close family member, the date you began your job, etc. All these are special and significant days in your life. Mark the month and lunar day for these dates, and anytime you want to start making any of the symbols described, choose one of these days, as they are not only important landmarks in your life but also special energy points as well.

In the sky, you can see one major source of energy, which is the sun. The sun is the significator of life; it provides critical energy for life to exist on earth and resonates with the life force in us. The moon resonates with the water content on earth, which is visible on the night of the full moon and dark night. Similarly, our everyday emotions are controlled by the moon.

In any month, there are three special days when the energy of the universe is resetting. As you get more sensitive towards the energy of space, your body will tell you that something is different in the energy on these days. This is because, on these days, either the sun, the moon or both of them are going through energy changes in their cycles.

One such day is around the 15th of every month, which is called Sankranti when the sun changes and enters the new zodiac sign. At the time of entering into any new zodiac, there is a disturbance in the energy of the universe. It is advisable to make donations on this day, like in the Hindu custom. Donations of seasonal fruits, wheat flour, jaggery, etc., are given in temples, but one can always donate to different online causes every month. You can volunteer your time to clean beaches or teach a child or perform any act selflessly towards someone else.

The second important days in every month are those of the dark night and the full moon. The emotional body goes through changes on these nights, so a donation of rice pudding, also known as payasam or kheer, is to be done in a temple. What happens when this donation is done is that the significator of our soul, the sun, and significator of our mind, the moon, goes into a zero state and the energy levels change. This is the time when, if we make a donation, it takes away a lot of our negative energy from the soul and mind, which we have acquired over a period of time.

The sun is considered the king of the zodiac and the principal entity for providing energy and life on earth. If we can get synchronized with the principal source of energy, then the rest of the energy sources will be easy.

Below, I have listed a general guideline based on the movement of the sun in the zodiac for the tasks you can do in a particular month.

**15 January–15 February:** Solving problems related to career, starting a savings account, working on pending tasks and objectives with complete dedication. The energy is of completing a task even if it requires strict discipline and actions.

**15 February–15 March:** Focus on family, make more connections, family functions. The energy is of enjoyment and reaping the fruit of hard work.

**15 March–15 April:** Clearing old debts, selling of any possession, charity. The energy is of giving out.

**15 April–15 May:** Child conception, working on health-related issues, overall personality development. The energy is to start anything new in life.

**15 May–15 June:** Accumulation of resources. The energy is to solve any kind of family dispute or internal doubts you have by talking to loved ones.

**15 June–15 July:** Learning new skills, initiation in a new school, creating online profiles on apps, sending proposals, paperwork, sibling or neighbour issues to be sorted during this time period.

**15 July–15 August:** Property-related matters, working for masses, making peace with situations. Any problems related to heart, lungs.

**15 August–15 September:** Taking new office, love life initiatives, government or management-related tasks, self-learning, making long-term plans, stomach-related ailments, celebrations, branding yourself.

**15 September–15 October:** Overall health-related problems, enemies. Try to resolve debts during this month and avoid any kind of partnership or new associations.

**15 October–15 November:** Marriage, relationships, partnership, business, travel for vacation.

**15 November–15 December:** This is a time for detox and transformation. This is a period when all rituals are related and when you need to let go of all grudges in life and consume a lot of antioxidants. It needs to be a physical as well as a spiritual detox. Let go of old things, guilt, shame and all those feelings which were unaddressed till now. This is the best time, as nature will support you and you can be lighter and ready for the next step of higher knowledge.

**15 December–15 January:** Making long-term plans and goals, initiating a search for higher knowledge of the universe, going to a guru or father to seek advice.

Once you choose your months to perform certain tasks, then you can choose from the cycle of the moon.

**New Moon:** Starting new ventures, moving to a new house, undertaking new projects.

**2nd Lunar Day:** Singing, dancing, eating out, buying groceries, stocking up items, money-related activities, meeting family members.

**3rd Lunar Day:** Travelling, writing, signing deals, paperwork.

**4th Lunar Day:** This is not a good day to start anything new, but it is a good time to let people go, buy electronics items, start meditation.

**5th Lunar Day:** Good for every activity except dealing with financial matters.

**6th Lunar Day:** Entering a new home, office, good for all fashion-related shopping, craft-related work.

**7th Lunar Day:** Good day for marriages, relationships, meeting new partners.

**8th Lunar Day:** Writing assignments, mining, research work.

**9th Lunar Day:** Initiating war or allegations.

**10th Lunar Day:** Starting new projects and getting praise and recognition in your work.

**11th Lunar Day:** Healing; medical ailments.

**12th Lunar Day:** Good for buying vehicles, banking work.

**13th Lunar Day:** Good for meditation and working selflessly, but not good for travel.

**14th Lunar Day:** Good for spiritual upliftment and doing penance.

**Full Moon Day:** Good for submitting final reports and closure reports.

## Got Energy—What's Next?

When you start getting energy from the universe, will all of you get the same results?

Do you get the same output when you plug in equipment in an electrical socket? The answer is no. Depending on the internal wiring of the equipment, you will get the necessary output, such as when you plug in a mixer, it rotates, whereas when you plug in your phone, the output is electricity to charge your phone. This is because different equipment have different internal wiring. Similarly, when you attract any energy from space, depending on your internal wiring, each one of you will have different results and some of you will feel confused as this was not what you were expecting to happen. There are instances when people suddenly lose their jobs after trying a yantra experiment.

Each one of us has a different way of handling energy in our bodies. The energy principle is that it follows the path of least resistance. Similarly, in your body, energy will follow the path of least resistance. If a certain passage is completely blocked in your life because of ego issues and short temper, for example, this means your stomach area energy is blocked and you will experience vomiting or dysentery and sudden health issues relating to this area coming up.

These issues are very common, as what is happening is that energy is trying to free your body from toxins. A healthy physical body is the first requirement to make you feel blissful. If in your life you have forgotten what waves of happiness are when you read something blissful, and how butterflies in the stomach go with happiness, it is only because not only on a physical level but also on a soul level, that energy chakra is blocked and therefore you are not able to experience the bliss.

Diseases like tuberculosis, cancer, IBS, heart blockages, etc., are ones that you have acquired over a long period of time. When you are unable to resolve issues on the soul level, then disease comes to the physical body. In the same way, when energy starts curing your soul, it will start from the physical body. If you are suffering from any long-term ailments such as diabetes and blood pressure, then for sure expect that a full detox of the body is going to happen in various ways. The liquid which comes out from the body in this process of cleansing will have an extremely bad smell.

Once your system gets cleansed, it might take up to fifteen days, but you will feel much lighter and different. Healing of the physical body will start first, and the medicine you have been taking will give you better results with reduced dosages.

## Cleansing the Physical Body

Since our own body is going to play a vital role in this process, it is important that we start preparing our body to absorb this energy. One of the most important ways to do this is through the decomposition of dead cells in the body.

Japanese biologist Yoshinori Ohsumi got the Nobel Prize for doing research on dead cells of the human body. Our body continuously generates new cells but what Ohsumi was interested in finding out was what happens to the dead cells in the body. During his research, he found out that these dead cells remain in the body until our body consumes them. This means that when we are hungry and the body requires food, it is the dead cells which are used, and the remaining extra dead cells in the body will result in diabetes, cancer and other diseases.

It is important that we fast at least twice a month, or ideally once a week. This is when we give up traditional food and consume only fruits once a day or go on a liquid diet so that we can decompose dead cells. When we eat light food, it is easier for the energy in our body to flow without disturbance. On the other hand, when we eat food to a point when the stomach is heavy, all the energy has to focus on the digestion of food. So even if you are in an energy zone with all the symbols, you will not be able to absorb any energy, as your body is not ready.

## Cleansing the Emotional Body

Once your physical body is ready, then you can move on to cleansing your emotional body. Your body will have resistance to energy due to negative emotions. This ritual for cleansing the emotional body will make it easier for you to connect to energy and channel it properly.

Humans have a habit of storing a lot of grudges and pain within them. Below, you will see how stored pain can affect you. At this point, I want you to perform a ritual of forgiving people and letting the pain go. There are people in your life who may have caused you suffering in the past and you might still hold grudges against them. You may feel emptiness as you have suffered the loss of loved ones. But what these memories do in your life is that they create a blockage in the energy circle. When you start receiving energy, these blockages will act as obstacles in the energy flow.

It is difficult to forgive people, but until and unless you forgive and move on, you will never be able to progress in life. The best way to do this is to hold a fruit, or some money or a flower in your hand. Then, sit down in one place and consciously let go of all the bad memories and experiences that are holding you back. This will help you let go of grudges, as this is a peace offering to everyone who has given you any kind of pain.

The remedy of holding a fruit, a flower or some money in your hand and saying 'I forgive you' and donating this in the name of the person who is ruling your head will have an amazing effect within fifteen minutes. All you need to do is pay attention, and you will see energy getting manifested. This is a ritual which you should do at least once in six months.

We all get multiple heads, like Ravan. There are many people who live in your mind rent-free and constantly block your progress. It can be your ex-partner, ex-employer, people who have not treated you right—and because of that you are not able to let go.

Even when Prabhu Ram was standing in front of Ravan, the king of Lanka was not able to receive light because a wall of ego was blocking it. Prabhu Ram was fighting but with compassion; he never showed hate, jealousy or complained to *bhagya*. Hate is one thing that will block all your routes forward towards success. That is why forgiving others is the most important thing you can do, in the same way as we forgive our own mistakes. The more compassionate we become in life, the more we start to receive blessings.

You can also do the ritual by holding something else as a peace offering, like a tree branch. Say, 'I forgive you all', from the heart. Remember, by keeping grudges you hurt yourself the most. You may feel like crying while doing this, and that is fine, as all the pain of leaving or being left by someone was inside you, and you were trying to be all right with so much hurt and bitterness inside you. You should never feel guilty for someone else's karma. There will be many people who come and go in our lives. This is because everyone has different stops in life where they need to get off.

# 7

# A Red Bicycle

Pain never goes away from our body if we don't address it. All the experiences of this life and past lives are stored. We, as humans, have mastered the art of ignoring and not paying attention to our own pain. We sometimes end up resorting to such things as alcohol or keeping our brain busy with something else so as to ignore the real issue going on within us.

Let me tell you about my own experience with this. I had a pain in my shoulder that was so bad, I was unable to lift my arm above a particular height. No medicine or physiotherapy was having any effect. After three months of going to every doctor in the city, I decided to have a look at my birth chart and I deciphered that, by August 2021, I will get some relief. But the pain was unbearable, and I was unable to even turn while sleeping.

**We never resolve our pain, we only ignore it. It is time to confront our pain and resolve our issues.**

Eventually, it was one of my students who solved the problem. One day, while teaching, I told the class that my shoulder will be all right in August as I could see the transit position. However, the pain was quite severe.

My student does past life regression, and she asked me if she could do a small energy cleansing for me. I was very reluctant, as past life regressions sometimes make you see a lot of bad things which have happened in the past and I was not ready for it. But I agreed finally, and my student told me, 'At the age of eight, there was a red toy which was taken away from you and that pain is now coming back as the issue was not resolved.' She added, 'Why not gift a red toy to a child? When a child plays with a similar toy, that will resolve the issue.'

**Some incidents cause us so much pain that even after we grow up, seeing certain things reminds us of it, as that hurt is still accumulated in our body.**

I was not able to recall anything about a red toy, but later on, I remembered an incident related to a red cycle which had disturbed me deeply when I was a child.

My student was able to make me recall this. When I gifted a red cycle to someone, the intense pain—which had not gone away even after several therapy sessions and medicines—finally went away by gifting joy to someone.

The pain which I had accumulated several years back appeared in the form of shoulder pain. I explained the astrological reasons on my blog as to why this had happened after so many years. Similar pain can be felt from time to time and creates problems which are beyond the understanding of medical science, and which cannot be helped by painkillers and physiotherapy.

Some pain is so deeply embedded in our lives that we don't even know it exists. When we look at certain things which remind us of bad memories, we become uncomfortable. In my case, it was an incident related to a red bicycle. Now, it is time for us to resolve these issues so that we can live a happy, worry-free life.

# 8

# One-Person Syndrome—The Superpower in You

Have you ever seen a movie like *Superman* or *Wonder Woman*? In the beginning, these people resist becoming a superheroes; they do not want to accept the mission they've been given. This is the story of each one of us, as none of us want to accept our superpowers. That is when the universe starts giving you problems in life so that you can sit in silence in grief and happiness and understand what your superpower is. Imagine a person gets rejected from a very well-paid job and he begins to make guitars, which eventually go on to sell for thousands of dollars.

In the Yajurveda, when gods were asking for special weapons to fight with, the crux of the story was, 'The weapons lie within you. You need to tap into powers hidden beneath the core.' I call it a one-man syndrome, as this is how profound this syndrome is. It makes you a genius on your own, the moment you decide to unleash the power hidden inside you.

We all look for help outside. We look for a guide, a mentor, a friend all the time, someone who can guide us through difficult times. This is due to a tendency that we are born and brought up with, in an environment where we are addicted to taking directions, orders and advice for every single thing. Firstly, most of the time, the person you are asking for help from will not be useful. The person will not be able to understand your circumstances and the context like you do. Their judgement will be based on the limited information that you are providing. Secondly, the person might give you advice but finally, it is you who has to face the consequences of each action. So instead of asking for help from anyone outside, you should try to solve your problems yourself.

Let me give you the wisdom of a person who trained in the Royal Air Force for twenty-two years and twenty-one days. He used to mention it every time. He would introduce himself as my 'Flying Instructor'.

'It was my first trip as a trainee on board, and after practising on simulators, it was time for hands-on flying experience. One day I noticed that the air conditioner of the control cabin was not working, so I went to the supervisor and informed him about it. This was the conversation between us.

Me: Dave, the aircon in the control cabin is not working.

Dave: So? Fix it.

Me: Should I fix it?

Dave: No. Let me call customer care and tell them to send a technician 150 miles out into the sea to fix a damn AC because we have got an engineer on board who is unable to fix some electrical equipment. Fix it or work in the heat.

'So, it came down to a point where either I had to fix the aircon on my own or work in the scorching heat of the sea. At that moment, my brain switched to the realization that no help was coming. There is some kind of superpower that kicks off in you, and you stop being dependent on anyone else. This helps your brain to stop looking elsewhere and focus on getting the task completed.

'Stop being dependent on other people. You are alone in this world and no one, and I repeat no one, will stand by your side if you are not worth their time and attention. People stay with us only until they see some benefit of their own. The moment you stop being useful, you will be replaced. It may sound rude to you but remember that you need to work on yourself. Instead of being dependent on anyone else, focus on how you can deal with the problem. The moment you unleash this superpower of solving problems, not only will you attract a lot of other people around you, but you will also gain respect from others. The sun burns itself to give life to others; that is why in the life of a king, moksha is not an option.

'As soon as I fixed the aircon, I was asked for help to fix a few more aircons that were not working on the vessel. The best part was that when I fixed the aircon in the kitchen, I not only made new friends but also enjoyed the best meals during the whole trip.'

One of the mantras which gives confidence and reminds you of who you truly are is: 'Aham Brahmasmi', meaning 'I am the universe'. Say it several times throughout the day and you will realize that the universe starts opening towards you.

There will be times when you will not be aware of how to complete a task. But you can always learn; there is nothing in this universe that you cannot learn and master.

We tend to look to someone else to pick us up and tell us what is good or bad in life. We need someone else's attention to give us that push and motivation in life. Often, people tend to ignore the problem until it becomes too late to act. I think we understand that there are a few things in life which we already know are bad for us, but we wait for someone else to push us to become great. We are always waiting for someone else to wake us up. It is human psychology that you want to do it the easy way: expecting that someone will come and tell you that these things are bad for you and those things will help you become great. We all know that drinking too much tea will spoil our liver, or by not exercising enough we are going to invite many diseases. We tend to ignore these things as much as possible, till one fine day we realize that we have so many issues and then we panic. We can correct this. I have a plan for you in the next chapter.

# 9

# Connecting to the Core

Once you have established that you are all alone and there is no help coming to save you in any situation, then congratulations, you are now on your path to becoming a legend, as you can now unleash the superpowers in you. But this book is not to motivate you to do great things to impress the world, but to make sure every single day you wake up with the feeling that you are a special child of God, who has been blessed with extraordinary superpowers.

Once you are isolated from the outer world, you can go inside your core and work on your powers. In ancient times, all saints used to have their ashrams outside the city, somewhere deep in the jungle. They knew that to achieve something great, one needed to live in isolation. We can think deeply about the secrets of the universe and are capable of performing extraordinary tasks by developing medicines, looking into the future, time travel and all other things mentioned in the Vedas.

To know your superpower, you have to go into silence, as every single piece of information you take in has to be processed by the brain and this requires vital energy of the brain. As mentioned earlier, when we travel on a train or a bus we feel dizzy after some time if we are constantly looking outside the window because we are taking in so much information through our eyes that our brain feels dizzy. Similarly, if you keep on wasting the vital energy of your brain on useless information from TV shows, phone calls or useless chats with people, your brain will not have enough power to give you a deep understanding of any subject. You will be left in life with no vision, and be prone to depression and failures. So, isolation is the key. Make sure you cut out all unnecessary information which is coming to you via the five senses so that you can experience what is in the hidden core inside you. The moment you start cutting down information going to your brain, mostly by visuals, your brain will send you signals of insecurity that there is something wrong today. Now you have disturbed the security algorithm of the brain.

You check your phone and different applications because your brain is sending you signals at regular intervals that something can go wrong. As humans, we have deep insecurities embedded in us. As part of the process of evolution, we have gone through periods where humans would get killed by animals, hunger and various natural causes. Today's world is much more secure and comfortable as compared to earlier.

If you compare the facilities you have provided for your children to the ones you had when you were growing up, you can see that they are better off now. But at every moment you are concerned about their security. These days, there are CCTVs in schools and their buses. Humans are obsessed with providing a secure environment.

Your fear is exploited by phone apps which ping you at regular intervals to tell you that something important has happened. Please check if someone has tagged you, poked you or commented on you. Because of your insecurity, you go ahead and spend a good amount of time on your phone which results in a draining of energy.

Remember this line: *The world makes money through fear or guilt.*

The more of these two components you add to your business, the more money and popularity your business will have. You cannot sell a product without these two components. Every industry works on this logic, and the moment you realize this, you stop being a part of the game. So, once you let go of your distractions, you can remain focused on important tasks for the day. You can now connect to your core internal power and the moment you connect to your inner world, something like magic kicks in. Now you have this feeling of happiness about everything in life, as you are living in the present. This feeling is the next step once you have removed the unnecessary information from your life.

I realized the happiness of living without much information while working on a ship. It was an eighty-six-day trip in the Indian Ocean, where the only way to communicate with the outside world was by satellite phone. This was accessible for only two to three minutes in a day, so I used to write letters home. During this time, I realized that I barely had any thoughts or dreams. I started looking at the sea for hours. Sitting alone at night for inspiration, I started remembering things from the past that were hidden deeply in my brain. This was not only surprising for me, but also a new experience.

This was the time when I realized that if any information was important enough, I would come to know about it, and that I don't need to check my phone, mail or news every fifteen minutes. This realization made a huge impact on me as it made me more secure and confident from within. There was a sense of relief from the inside to live a life where importance was given to my soul rather than other people's lives on Facebook or irrelevant news where people were trying to push their agenda to brainwash society. I did make the important decision to get off any app which sent me notifications every hour or distracted me from enjoying the moment. Till date, I don't have any popular apps on my phone, as I don't want to be notified about anything.

People are so busy with their phones that they have forgotten to love their children and feel the joy of being with their loved ones. If you are distracted in life, then you can't focus on love or work, or give your 100 per cent to what you are doing. You are only living a half-life, as in the other half you are already virtual.

To test this, ask yourself when you are clicking a photograph if the thought is already running in your head of posting it on social media. If you answered yes, then you clicked that photograph for social media and not for yourself. And the reason you are doing so is because you need approval in the form of likes and comments. Your inner core does not have the contentment of being satisfied with who you really are. You require someone else to satisfy this need for appreciation. Virtual likes and comments are a distraction and unnecessary information that does not let you connect to people deeply. Then how is it possible that this virtual world will allow you to connect to your inner core?

# 10

# Energy from the Universe

Once you have learnt to live with a minimum amount of information in your life and started focusing on yourself more than on the outside world, it will be easy for you to get connected to nature and receive energy from the five elements of life, as described in the earlier chapters.

Everything in our life is a by-product of energy. Look around you and analyse your life. Whatever you have acquired in life till now and wherever you have reached till now is only due to the energy you have gathered from the universe. If you are suffering from health issues, a bad marriage or money-related troubles, these are the forms of energy you have attracted in life. There is nothing in this world which works beyond the principle of energy.

At this point in the book, I am asking you to trust me as I have followed every single ritual written in the book. I am telling you this from practical experience that once you start attracting the right energy in your life, life will move like magic. You will have experiences which are not explicable to anyone and only you can see the magic happening. This includes seeing events beforehand in dreams and a feeling of déjà vu throughout your life.

You will have thoughts about something in the morning, like a song, a person, a requirement of something, and by evening the same opportunities will be presented to you on a platter. You will be the right person at the right time due to energy synchronization in your life. This will go to a level where you feel that you have a direct connection with God. You will also have the feeling of holding power when things happen smoothly in business and your personal life, just by thinking about them. You will be presented with opportunities from people that you never expected. These things will happen quite often.

The only precaution is to keep your goal higher, as sometimes you yourself don't believe that you deserve more than what you are getting. Remember that the universe has an abundance of energy. When it starts delivering the burst of energy, you will not even be able to imagine what the universe can provide you.

Imagine you wake up every morning and you have no idea as to what gifts you will receive today from nature and who will walk into your office with which particular opportunity. All this is happening as you have created an energy around you which has attracted various unseen forces towards you.

A lot of people do various types of penance to achieve things. What they have not been told is that the secret lies within you and, once you activate it, you don't need to go to the jungle and do penance for smaller things in life. Once you understand the principle of energy in life and how you can move up by balancing the energy, nothing is going to stop you from becoming great and achieving the things you want in life.

The law of manifestation only works for a few people and not for everyone. The reason is that some people have a good amount of energy, and it is easy for them to attract whatever they want. But for some people this doesn't work at all. Otherwise, all of us will start getting what we wish for, and the world will only consist of rich people.

It is the law of energy that energy flows on a path of least resistance and when there is resistance of various kinds or any kind of trouble in the circuit, the energy prefers to travel elsewhere. The same thing happens in the universe. The universe wants to deliver energy to you. It wants to talk to you and explain the secrets by giving you enough signals to make you understand that every single moment the universe is with you. But it is also looking for the path of least resistance. The universe is also looking for your attention and silence so it can talk to you. But until and unless you learn to isolate yourself and go into your inner core, the universe will give you sparks but you will not be able to identify this power.

## Ritual of Open Sky

Let us now introduce you to the magic of the universe through rituals, which I have not only personally tried but also introduced to several clients to get connected to the energy sources.

One of the ways to start sending your vibrations to the universe and receive healing from the universe is by sending messages when the sky is open. What I mean by an open sky is that there is a particular time period when energy from the sky is at its maximum. Scientists also confirm that during a particular time period, there is a maximum amount of energy variation in the sky.

The beauty of this ritual is that you can do it anywhere in the world and you will feel the effect.

Choose one of these time periods: in the morning when the sun is about to come up and you can still see stars in the sky, or every evening when the two time periods meet again, known as the zero time period of the day. If possible, you can do this exercise twice a day. Go to a terrace or balcony or a place where you can see the sky, and now start mentally sending out all your plans into the sky.

Now what happens during this period is that the sky is in reset mode, and this is the time when both energy sources are visible in the sky. So, what happens during this time period is that you start receiving energy from space. This is the energy of calmness. If you notice the sea during the early morning or around evening, you will realize that time has come to a standstill and achieved a zero state. This is when the sky is downpouring energy on earth and, if at this point of time you are standing on the roof looking at the sky with a dream in your mind, this energy is going to help you to achieve it by helping you in unexpected ways.

Let me give you a real-life example. A lady approached me for consultation and her email, I felt, was different from other emails I've received. In her email, she mentioned that within two years of her marriage, her husband had passed away a in road accident. Subsequently, she was facing a crisis. She was living in her parents' home with a small child and no certainty about her future. In order to help her I took her birth chart for reading and realized that if she could manage the ether element in her chart, she would be able to do quite well in life. So, I asked her to do this ritual for a month without fail and give me her feedback on what had changed.

She came back in fifteen days with some news. As her husband had died in a road accident, one of their friends had filed for an insurance claim, which she was not even aware of. She received a cheque from the insurance company, and the amount was quite large. I asked her to continue with the ritual and keep giving me updates. In three months, this lady's life changed. She had done a beautician's course from a reputed school before her marriage. She applied for a franchise from the same school, which she got. She was now running a beauty parlour along with a boutique. This was the time she offered to pay me for this wonderful ritual.

Can you see what has happened here? How one simple ritual had changed her life? This was not a unique case, and I was not even excited or surprised to see this kind of result. I have seen this happening so many times that magic has become normal for me. That is why I am telling you that the universe does magic every day, but we are too busy in our mundane lives to notice it. All I am asking you is to feel it by doing it yourself. Until and unless you experience the energy of the universe yourself, you will not know what you are missing in life.

Sometimes, you need a new start in life, as you want to get out of the daily mundane routine where you have always been stuck. To get out of the endless loop, you need a zero state. Every morning and evening the universe resets itself by bringing two different energies at the same time in the sky. If you receive this energy, you will also experience a state of reset in your life.

This ritual also helps to tackle negative emotions which are deeply embedded in us, by providing us energy to achieve a zero state of emotion. Soon you will realize that your outlook towards life is changing because now when you are receiving the new energy, the clutter inside you is getting clean. You will feel more relaxed and full of new thoughts every day. You will feel motivated to move ahead in life and do new things. Whatever grudges or pre-conditioning of your brain that were holding you back are now removed, and you can think with an open mind.

As humans, we are more biased towards negative information, rather than positive things in life. It is with this negative conditioning that humans are brought up. Your brain is programmed in a manner which gives attention to negative information rather than to positive. What the negative bias does to the brain is that it makes you psychologically weak. This is because you are already programmed that something will go wrong in life, and sooner or later it manifests easily.

You could receive a thousand positive comments, and you will be happy, but your brain is a master at ignoring all the good comments and focusing instead on the one negative comment you got at a party that you have not been able to forget. As Osho ji said, even after drinking nectar a thousand times, you only require one drop of poison to kill anyone.

## Pandora of Emotions

Water is a major component of the human body, any ritual that you do that involves water will affect you the most. In Hinduism, there is a saying that life begins with water and ends with water. When Hindus die, their ashes are thrown into a river so that they can continue their journey into the next life easily and attain moksha.

Water has the property to store information, and it does this in the form of feelings. You see people who don't sweat despite working hard. These people get problems not only at the physical level but at the emotional level as well. That is why it is necessary to sweat when exercising for a healthy brain and soul.

If there are a maximum number of rituals for any element, then it is for water, as it helps to cleanse at different levels. This takes time, and the more you cleanse your water body, the more you will see the shine in your face coming through. You will feel lighter every moment and your energy levels will shoot up. Tears, urine, sweat, blood flow, brain liquid and every portion of your body has water; it controls the important functions. We need to continuously work on how we energize the water element in the body.

Have you ever wondered why we take a shower? Water gives you a feeling of being fresh and energetic by providing you with energy. Water has to provide us energy to refresh us, but are we really getting energized water? In the early days, people used to get their water from natural sources. This was water which was stored in the form of ice for several hundred years, so the moment you drank it or took a shower in it, you felt refreshed. But nowadays, when water has been recycled from sewage, very little natural energy is left in the water.

So, we will start by charging our water every time we are going to use it. You will see the result of this ritual very clearly in your levels of happiness and calm. You will start realizing that, if you were suffering from any disease which you thought was impossible to cure, such as psoriasis, diabetes or even cancer, it is better within a week and your medicine has become more effective than before.

The ritual is simple: we need to programme the water in which we are going to take a bath, which is going to cleanse us, and it is a fun exercise to quickly lighten the mood and relieve stress. The ritual is, even before you enter to take a shower, decide on a song you are going to sing, and then sing with complete emotion. It can be a devotional bhajan, it can be a romantic song, but it should come from your heart. You will eventually realize that this is such a brilliant remedy to cleanse yourself every day.

Let me share an email with you from a person who was suffering from a skin allergy in the private parts and the groin area. Even after regular treatment this was spreading and was becoming a source of embarrassment for the person. I could see in the birth chart that his water element was imbalanced and creating issues on the mental plane. I asked him if he was irritated about certain things in his life or if there was any lingering issue that he was unable to solve, such as some emotional turmoil he was going through. This gentleman had recently changed his job, but he was still holding a grudge against his old company. This resentment was coming out in the form of this skin infection.

Diseases always start at a mental level first, whether it is thyroid, cancer or diabetes. We only find out about our disease when it starts harming the physical body. When you deprive your emotional body of soul food, these problems will appear in your body. The next time you have any negative feelings, ask yourself how you can correct them. Your brain can bring heaven to earth if you ask yourself questions such as: Why do I have anger towards anyone? Why am I not happy? What's bothering me? How can I live a happier life? Can I solve the core issue of my heart?

Trust me, you will get answers when you seek them, rather than draining your energy with negativity and inviting diseases into your life. The universe answers questions when you seek them. Start by cultivating new routines that cleanse you every day and take away negative emotions so that you can live in peace.

Here is a feedback email I received one week after the person tried the ritual I suggested:

Dear Deepanshuji,

Some kind of miracle has happened, 90% of my skin has cleared.

You are a precious gift for us Sir. I pray to God to keep you and your family, especially your children, safe and happy forever . . .'

All this happened because he trusted my wisdom and balanced the elements by performing the ritual I suggested. You too can experience the same by connecting yourself to the energy of water.

## Activating Chakras by Water

There are seven energy points in our body known as chakras. These are basically power centres to provide us with energy throughout the day.

These chakras hold an enormous amount of power and are able to receive and send energy to the universe. However, most people have these chakras working at a minimum level, as they do not work to activate these chakras and use the energy of the universe. These are the seven energy reactors in your body, and you need to activate them by various means. One of the simplest methods is by taking a cold-water shower. This can be difficult for people who are used to taking hot showers. What happens when you take a cold-water shower is that the temperature difference between your body and the water makes you very uncomfortable. As a result, your body is now suddenly activated to counter this cold by various means internally. In this process, suddenly all of your inner body, which is called 'Sookshma Sarir' or the micro body, wakes up all the chakras to provide you with energy. Now the whole day your energy levels will be on a different level. This also activates your brain, increases the immunity level and you will see the difference from day one; every day your energy will continue to increase.

I came across an interesting video on YouTube. There is a city in Russia called Yakutsk, where the temperature goes as low as -50° Celsius. In this city, there is a sixty-year-old person, Nikolai, who takes a bath in the freezing waters of a frozen lake. I came across a video on YouTube where he explains that he has done this every day for the last thirty years. He grew up falling sick a lot when he was a child, but in these last thirty years, he has never fallen sick or had to visit a doctor. Now his internal immunity is activated every morning, killing all the cancer cells or any other kind of diseases which might be developing inside him.

Visible health benefits are one part, but this ritual of taking a cold-water shower is to activate your energy points in your body so that your awareness around you will increase. You can take a hot water shower only when you are trying to sleep and that too just before sleeping, but not in the morning.

## Moving on—A Ritual of Goodbye

The most painful goodbyes are the ones which are never spoken. Water holds emotions and it is emotional pain which damages us the most. Sometimes we need to say a final goodbye to a job, city, person, etc. It can be anything in your life which you want to be liberated from so that everyone can carry on with their journey.

The ritual is simple but effective; several people who have tried this have experiences that they would never believe. There was a court case between brothers over a division of business and no conclusion was coming for the last several years. When one of the brothers performed this remedy not only was the division finalized in a week with mutual agreement, but relations also returned to normal. This ritual can give extraordinary results.

On a special day, like your birthday, anniversary, a dark night, a full moon night, etc., go to a water body and make an offering of some fruits, dry fruits, a mirror and some copper coins. When the cosmos has energy, water is more responsive on those days. This can be seen in the tides of the sea as well.

Now say your prayers mentally like I did once as I was tired of spending two hundred days in a year on a ship. I took a bag of dry fruits and said a prayer saying that I am done with the sea, and I do not wish to come back here, so here is my final offering to you. Now please do not call me back. I felt there was an energy which was calling me back again and again to the sea but, surprisingly, that was my last trip offshore. I was meant to visit the open sea twice after that. But something supernatural happened both times, and the ship was not able to leave the port with me. I realized that my karma with the sea was now over.

We all have a karma with everyone around us. There may be a reason why the sea was calling me. The fish in the sea may have had a karma with me, as I used to feed them regularly. Everyone in our life stays with us until their karma with us is over. Once we nullify that debt of the past life, people go away from our life.

This ritual is like asking for a rebate from the universe. Imagine you borrowed Rs 1000 from someone and you have already paid Rs 800 but now for the rest you pray that you have to only give Rs 100 more and be allowed to carry on your journey. Nature is kind enough to let that happen.

There may be an ex-spouse who is still holding you back and you may not be able to move on with your life. The best way to deal with this is to go to a water body on your anniversary and ask for it to be let go. Say that this is all I have now for you, let me carry on my journey, I am tired of this. When you pray from a genuine and truthful space in your heart, then magic happens in the universe. You will suddenly see the ball rolling in your favour. I have seen so many emails citing the miracles that have happened each time any of my clients have done these remedies.

## Switching to a King Mentality

I will ask you to do a ritual which will make you not only shine like a bright star but will also help you to complete the journey of your soul. Usually, people use this term 'soul desire', but in reality very few of them know what the true desire of the soul is, as the soul does not have the ability to express things. The soul always requires the *atman* to express desires.

One of the simple rituals you can follow is to look at the sun as it rises in the sky, when it is orange in colour. You will realize within a few days that you are getting opportunities to do work which you have only dreamt of till now. When you wake up early and watch the rising sun, something changes in your brain, as the energy levels of the brain and the body are on different levels. At any point of time, you radiate energy and, depending on your aura, it is either positive or negative energy. The way people treat you is based on this energy.

Sometimes this energy is so disturbed that it makes you wonder why, after all your hard work, you are not getting any success. The reason is you are radiating extremely negative energy which you have accumulated. We can turn this into positive energy by accumulating positive energy through performing rituals. Start by looking at the rising sun, but the condition is that do not ask for anything, as the sun being the significator of the soul knows better than you. All you have to do is look at the rising sun and let the universe do the magic for you.

I see people who are lost in their lives; they have no clue as to who they truly are and instead of thinking of what they can do for the world, these people are thinking of what they can take from the world. I realize that these people require the energy of the soul. As your soul has taken birth to become one of the greatest in the world, do not worry about matters which are artificially created for you.

The moment you decide to be in a mode of *what can I give to others*, at that very moment you have switched to the mentality of a king. There are very few people in this world who live with this mentality. There are very few people in the world who can say these golden words—'How can I help you?'—with true intention behind them. These are very powerful words, but some people use them as a part of their jobs every day. Less than 1 per cent use them with the intention of truly helping people in need.

The universe has everything in abundance, whether it be money, health, wisdom, houses, etc. You name anything, and the universe has it, but why do only a few become rich, famous and blessed with so many superpowers? The answer lies in the intention. Nature wants to give you all of these, and it searches for people through whom it can deliver its work. For instance, if nature wants to feed a hundred families who have lost everything in a calamity, it sends signals to many people that day to help through donations. Only a few will pick up the signal and donate for the cause.

If you are one of those people who picked up the signal, the universe has now marked you as a person who is a giver, and as you had low resistance towards this intuition to donate, nature has marked you as a good conductor through which to get work done. YOU BECOME THE CHOSEN ONE.

Nature will bless you with more money and opportunities, with which you can travel and help many people in the world. You are only the medium to deliver the messages of the universe to different people. Imagine the frustration of the universe, that it wants to deliver so much abundance, but it is difficult to find people and has to limit itself to 2 per cent only. Most humans are not ready to become a medium and want to be on the taker's end, rather than the giver's end.

Let me tell you how nature gives you resources when you use these golden words with pure intentions.

The universe has a rhythm and if you can get synchronized to the same rhythm as the universe, you will feel that life is easy and everything you desire gets manifested easily. The reason is that you are in the flow with the energy of the universe. But what is the rhythm of the universe? Ask yourself, if you own everything in this world, what will be your priority? If you can't think of that, then think on a smaller scale. What would be your priority as the head of a state or head of a city, or what might be your priority if you were the boss in your office?

You know that the topmost priority for any head is that every single person in their team should be able to do their job with perfection and without complaint. Secondly, they should be cooperative with other team members so that they can deliver projects on time. But imagine if, as a head, all you get to hear are complaints, conspiracies and the nagging attitude of people who want to somehow evade the job.

The rhythm of the universe is almost the same, and it searches for humans who can be grateful in life for the task assigned to them and can cooperate with other living beings to create a harmonious environment. Let me explain it to you more so that you can truly realize this and become more aware of your surroundings. At every point in time, you radiate an energy, and this energy is the energy of your thoughts. You can try this as an experiment: every day start your work by appreciating every single thing you are going to use. You will suddenly see that either some equipment will go bad in a few days, or you will start getting opportunities which you never thought would come.

Why would any equipment go bad when you were appreciating it? What happens is that when you start appreciating something there is a particular amount of negative energy inside you, which you have stored by criticizing many people and things, and when this energy goes out, it is absorbed by the most vulnerable equipment and it breaks down.

The Facebook group of Lunar Astro is filled with these miracles where people have experienced things which they had previously thought were unimaginable. As you continue to follow practices that align you with the universe, you will realize your energy circle is increasing and you will have a far better understanding of energy.

## Animal Instinct—Energy to Move in Life

You are in this world not as a single entity but as part of a large ecosystem—which includes animals, ghosts, humans. In the Rigveda, there is a prayer that everyone should get peace, the ones who are visible and the ones who are not visible. It means there are energies around us which are not visible to the naked eye, but they do exist in this world. There are several cases of people experiencing someone protecting them or harming them, but they are not visible.

If you want to see the true nature of any human, observe how they treat animals around them. Doing anything for animals is selfless as they can never pay you back by any means. The way someone treats animals reveals their true nature. Similarly, animals are more sensitive at sensing energies as they are closer to nature.

Let me share a short story of a friend. His family resided in a house in the outskirts of Punjab. A stray dog in a dirty condition used to come to the gate of their house in the hope of getting some food. This family used to shoo the dog away as they were afraid of its appearance. One night, the grandmother dreamt of her late husband, but instead of a human head, there was the head of a dog on her husband's body asking, *'Why are you people not letting me inside the house? I wasn't able to pay back the loan of Rs 50,000 which I took from a particular gentleman, that is why I am in this condition. Please pay Rs 50,000 to that person.'*

The grandmother told the family about her dream and then called the person that her husband had mentioned. This person was an old friend of the grandfather's. He said that he had given a loan to him as a friend. There was no paperwork so, once he passed away, the friend thought he would let it go as his time was also near.

The family paid the loan on the same day to the gentleman and welcomed the dog inside the house. They made a very comfortable bed for the dog. The same night the grandmother again had a dream, but this time her husband had a human head saying thank you. The next morning the dog was no more. It had passed away while sleeping.

Animals come into your life for a reason. You will see that animals do not respond to just everyone. They pick up vibrations and respond to the right one. The other day I was in a forest for an evening walk, and I saw a mountain dog. Its fur was pitch black, and it was big and scary as well. Out of the fifteen people there, this dog started playing with me, jumping around like he wanted to express his happiness. This was a dog that everyone else was calling, but he sensed a feeling of joy which I was experiencing, as I was in gratitude towards the universe.

All Hindu gods and goddesses in any depiction are always with animals. It is always mentioned that God has the ability to travel anywhere, anytime, defeating the concept of space and time. So why does God require an animal to travel on? Like vehicles help us to travel with ease from point A to B only when we have learned how to drive the car or bike and have control over its energy, similarly every Devta and Devi comes with a vehicle.

Animals come into our life to help us move from point A to B. All the gods are capable of moving freely anywhere, but they still have a *vahan* which helps them find their way and acts as a GPS—such as a rat for Ganeshji. A rat represents problems, and Lord Ganesh has mastered the art of managing problems. An owl is the vahan for Maa Laxmi, the goddess of wealth, to travel to a person without ego and anger. She uses the owl as it travels at night. Dogs are used by Bhairav, the fierce god of death. So, when any animal comes to your door, it is to guide you so that you can complete your journey.

The entry of these animals in your life shows that now you are ready for a change. So don't be afraid of them, as no animal is unlucky. It is just that, at a particular point of time, you require the energy of that particular animal only, just as you choose your car or bike according to the path and destination.

When you provide food, shelter or water to any animal, nature thanks you several hundred times for being the person who has taken care of another living creature. In return, animals absorb a great amount of negative energy from you to heal you. Animals have a special feature—they can absorb negative energy and dissipate it easily as they have control over this energy. Let us see what energy different animals carry. Some of them are domestic animals and some are wild. In the case of wild animals, you can get energy from them by watching a documentary on them or by placing a photograph or symbol of these animals near your desk.

Dogs absorb anxiety and fear from you and also take care of any litigation issues in your life. If you are unable to get a dog, then watch a documentary on them. In just two or three hours some positive news will arrive, as now you have started to discharge your energy towards the animal, which can handle it.

Cats absorb any emotional disturbance and take away any aggression building inside you. Cats avoid fighting unless it is absolutely necessary, as by getting into fights the main objective gets delayed as well. To find loopholes in any system when you are stuck in life, it is only cats that can help you.

The cow is considered a sacred animal as it absorbs the maximum amount of negative energy from humans and helps them to be in a harmonious relationship with everyone. In earlier days of human evolution, dairy animals were the security against droughts and floods. Cows bring resources and abundance in life.

Goats make you fearless and bless you with determination when you are at an important junction in your life. When you feel there are a lot of obstacles and hurdles coming in your life, then the energy of a goat is very useful.

Crocodiles make you patient, so you are able to wait for the right opportunities to arrive. They make you work and complete a task with patience, even when you see no positive sign of improvement in your life and have limited resources. It is the energy of a crocodile which helps you grab the right opportunity. Usually, people fail in life because they are unable to identify the right opportunity.

Lions make you a good planner, someone who makes the best use of resources. Their energy ensures you dominate the field you are in, by slowly and steadily leaving your marks around in the jungle. Any alpha will want to mark out their territory in the jungle, and they do so by urinating at different places to make sure everyone knows who the king is there. Even when a lion sleeps, there is a snoring sound loud enough to encompass the area. Sometimes when you are on top, some people will have the misconception that you achieved it by fluke or luck. But you should always remind other animals that the lion becomes the king of the jungle solely by his power, not by the 'mercy of hyenas'. Your competitors should never forget this.

Bulls show determination and resourcefulness. As a bull is a sign of raw power and masculinity, it is used in agricultural fields for ploughing. When you feel that you are all alone and need more support and power, then feeding a bull regularly will help.

Fish give you the energy to complete tasks and have happy endings, when you want to get rid of any particular person, job or city without confrontation.

We as humans have an instinct that guides us on approaching our life in terms of short-term goals. It is always the energy of animals that helps us quickly get out of any problems in life.

## Invisible Beings and Learning

When you want to learn something that has never been done before in this world, when you want to read things that have not been written, you need to connect yourself to the energy source of the universe, and you can do this by connecting to someone who has that knowledge but is not in this world.

We pray to different gods and goddesses for power as these gods and goddesses have mastered that energy in their lives and achieved the status of divinity. The energy of these deities will help us to get the right resources, motivation and guidance to complete our projects. Whichever field you are working in, whether it's arts or engineering or computers, to become a legend in that particular area you will require inspiration to move forward. If you are working in the sea, you should respect the god of water Varuna and ask him for help. But even if you don't know about Varuna, you can always pray to water and your ship. If you are in the arts and are not getting enough ideas, you should pray for the energies around you or visit an art gallery that has the works of your favourite painter. That art gallery will have the energy of the painter to give you the right direction.

*Lal Kitab*, a book by the late Pandit Roop Chand Joshiji, is considered one of the best manuscripts from which to learn the secrets of astrology. Whenever anyone asked Panditji who had written this book, his reply was always, 'Someone came to write this.' Every night in his dreams someone used to explain things to him and the next morning he would write in the book what had been explained to him.

One day, when Roop Chand Joshiji was writing, suddenly his son came running to him, telling him to change a particular line in the book. He wrote in *Lal Kitab* that *'now spirits are talking to my children as well.'* This book is very powerful as it carries energy which only a few can handle, as this book is written by spirits.

As I was reading this book, I started saying that this is a book of your past karma and what has been written in this book has a very different meaning. Rather than taking it in a literal sense, I faced huge opposition and was ridiculed by many. But I was sure about what I was experiencing.

For instance, one of the lines in this book is, 'flowers of the dead'. Astrologers understood this as a person will not have any future, like dead flowers. But when the energy of this book got channelized, I realized what is meant by flowers of the dead. It meant that the person had forgotten to pay his respects to dead people. That is why problems in his life will come. There are many more terms like this which give deep insights. But a time came when I felt frustrated and closed this book with disappointment and said until and unless you want me to learn this, I am not going to open it again.

That evening, I saw about ten emails from a student from Canada asking for my phone number to talk to me. I politely refused as most emails like this are from people who have an agenda to get a consultation somehow. Due to shortage of time, I refuse these requests. But this student was adamant. Finally, he wrote that this was about a dream he'd had about *Lal Kitab*, which he needed to tell me about. This was interesting for me. I wanted to hear more about the dream so I connected with him.

The person, Mr Rajiv, is settled in Canada and runs a software company. He started explaining how he knew the family of Pandit Roop Chand Joshiji and the history of *Lal Kitab*. Then he said something very shocking. He said that in his dreams he saw the late Pandit Roop Chandji asking him to hand over certain things to me.

Mr Rajiv had handwritten the book as well as bought the domain of Lal-kitab.com, which is a premium domain. The history of this domain was not pleasant as there had been court cases and fights over ownership of the domain name. But Rajivji had not sold or given it to anyone as this was the order of Panditji. But this time he was offering it to me as he had received orders to do so in his dream. At that point in time, I was running the website of Lunar Astro on a simple platform and didn't have much knowledge about domain transfers.

It was then that I realized what kind of power I was dealing with. In just a few hours the energy of this book had given results. This is how magical this universe is.

Similarly, when you read any book, you can feel the energy of the writer through it. If by reading this book you don't feel like dancing or get goosebumps, then you are not getting my energy.

When you practise any art or skill in life, you should pray for the person who has designed that skill and try to get connected to that person with a pure desire to learn. The universe will not only guide you but will also provide you with means in such unexpected ways that you will be surprised at how easy it is to learn something.

154

All learning and all knowledge is in space. The universe is searching for people in every area, every domain, for a master who can absorb that energy and lift everyone else up. When you do the work of nature, nature helps you, but you need to learn to download it. You need to be in the frequency of Da Vinci to learn the style of Da Vinci's paintings.

If you want to be the best healer or surgeon in this world, medical school can teach you procedures and impart knowledge, but what no one can teach is the ability to heal people. There are doctors who carry magic in their hands. Sometimes you realize that after you visit a doctor, before you even take the medicine, healing starts. The energy of the doctor is important. If the doctor is working only for money, they may be able to give you medicine but will not be able to heal you.

When you start crying for knowledge, when you want to be an absolute legend in your field, you need to have that magic in your art.

## City–Area–House

You cannot control where you are born but you can always choose a city, area or house to live in. Every city has a particular history and certain energy levels.

Based on this, your life will move up or down. When you were in school, your teachers would say, 'Show me your friends and I will tell you your future.' Similarly, when you move to a new city, find out what the city is famous for and whether its energy will suit you. When the great epic war Mahabharata had to take place, a person was sent in search of a land where the energy was so negative that even relatives would start hating each other. The war was between brothers and the place was Kurukshetra, where this epic battle took place. The energy of this place was so negative that when a devotee named Sravan Kumar was carrying his parents on his shoulders so that they could visit the Char Dhams, the moment they reached Kurukshetra, he asked his parents for money. Realizing that something had affected their son as he had never behaved in such a manner, the father asked him the name of the city that they were in. When he told them it was Kurukshetra, the parents said they would give him the money after crossing the city. The parents knew that it was the effect of the energy of the city, and after they crossed it, their son would be out of its spell.

Other battles have also been fought in the same region later on, like the Battle of Panipat.

So before moving to a city, always check what its history is, and then see if the energy suits you. For some people this energy will be useful in their journey but might not be useful for their progress. An industrial city is very mechanical and not good for education or creative purposes. But it may be good for staying focused in life, as you will see that the energy of the city is competitive. The energy of a city will attract the same kind of people, and you may not want to live in an environment where people are not like-minded.

Secondly, do a quick check of the area where you want to live. Take a good look around at the houses and the kind of life people are living there. Look at the cars in the driveway, how many happy couples did you see at any community gathering? See the overall landscape, the kind of products the local market is selling, whether it is upscale or just has the necessities. Some areas are deprived of energy, money, health and relationships. You will see that the moment you move to a neighbourhood where most people have bad married lives, you will experience the same.

It is very important to choose your flat or house in a society where happy people are living. There are some places where you feel angry and not good the moment you enter, whereas some places give you a feeling of belonging. This is only due to energy. The same energy will help you grow in life when you come back after a tiring day at office. There should be a feeling of happiness about returning home. Every time you see your house you should feel, 'I am home'. That is why you should take your time to find your dream house. The best way to ask for a dream house is to place a picture of your dream home as the wallpaper on your computer or as a painting. Then ask nature to let you drive to that dream house.

# 11

# Small Changes, Big Impacts

We must realize our shortcomings related to dependency, get back to life on our own and not wait for anyone's support in life. You cannot just get out of bed one day and say, I am going to be stronger and not be dependent on anyone else. If you are not going to follow a step-by-step process, most likely you are going to fail in a few days or a week at the most. This is because there is no goal you have set for yourself, and you have no idea what to do next. My suggestion is to make small changes in your daily routine. These small changes are going to ensure that you improve consistently and get more power and wisdom every day.

Small changes in your daily routine ensure that you experience a burst of energy. When we start making positive changes in life, a chemical reaction occurs in the brain which generates happiness, confidence and a feeling of self-contentment. This happiness motivates us further to make more self-corrections.

We will go into the details of the several changes you can bring into your life. But before we start, we need to do one simple exercise as part of our morning routine. Every morning, when you wake up, plan your day and your future. This is the time you should talk to yourself. Apart from this, you should start with simple exercises to take care of your health, and then add one good habit a week, such as waking up early, an evening walk, healthier food habits, etc. Small changes have a greater impact.

## Working for Greatness

All the happiness or misery you are in right now was once a small thought in your brain. So, programme your brain for greatness. You can achieve greatness by changing your motivation for work, as your level of motivation decides your happiness in that work. If you are passionate about what you do for work, that is the best, as you become a creator in that profession. There are very few people who enjoy their work and are not creative.

If you are not creative in your life, you will be tense and heavy in the head all the time as you are not enjoying what you are doing. Now you will need to discharge this energy via sex, alcohol or various other means. People who are extremely creative in their work usually have sexual desires which are not like animals. For them, that too becomes an art, as creative people want to enjoy every moment of what they do.

When you write a poem, that is being creative—and creativity cannot be utilized. Anything which can be utilized or written to impress others or to get praise is not creative. If I decode a dictum from a classical astrological book, it is because I love doing this. What I will get from it or what is the value of decoding that one line is nothing. No one knows the happiness or sadness of creativity.

When you work for your soul, your creativity comes out, and when you work for creativity, suddenly you are on a legendary level of work. Now whatever you are performing or doing, whether it is cooking food or cleaning the office, teaching or coding software, you are doing it as an artist with soul.

Earlier, you were working from fear rather than for your excellence. Fear is what can kill all your dreams. That is why you should continuously work against that fear.

## Deprivation of Food for the Soul

What will happen if you don't eat for two days? Most likely you will be grumpy or start running in search of food. As time passes you will get more desperate for food. But what if I told you that it is not only your human body but also your soul which requires food. If you don't provide food for the soul, you will start getting diseases and other problems.

Disease always starts at a mental level first, whether it is thyroid, cancer or diabetes. We only notice it when it starts harming the physical body. Similarly, when you deprive yourself of soul food, these problems will appear in your body.

When you learn something new, your brain generates happiness. People who don't learn new things get old and depressed over a period of time, as your brain requires that happiness constantly.

Your everyday routine will decide your long-term achievements. Every single day, when you work towards the impossible goal that drives you, don't deprive yourself of soul food. Ask yourself questions. Next time you have negative feelings, ask yourself how you can correct it. Your brain can bring heaven on earth if you ask yourself questions such as: Why do I have hatred issues? Why am I not happy? What's bothering me? How can I live a happier life? Can I solve the core issues of my heart?

Trust me you will get answers when you seek them rather than draining your energy in negativity and inviting diseases into your life. The universe answers questions when you are seeking them. Start by cultivating new routines which are cleansing you every day, such as mantra *jaap*, going to the temple every day and doing havan once a week or every fifteen days. These rituals will keep your unnecessary desires in control and keep inspiring you to do something for the greater good. We see the world through our eyes but understand it from our hearts. It takes the heart of a lover, a child or a devotee to see the magical universe.

Once, Buddha was meditating in a jungle on a full moon night. In the same jungle, there were some drunkards who were in search of a beautiful woman there. They asked Buddha, 'Have you seen any beautiful woman passing by?' Buddha replied, 'I don't know whether the person who passed by was a male or a female as sometimes I am male or female depending on my understanding of myself.'

These men were really confused with Buddha's answer and said again that the woman who passed by was very beautiful. Buddha replied that 'beauty' depends on what you want to see.

This is absolutely correct, for what seems beautiful for one person might be ugly to someone else. It is your own understanding of beauty which lies within you; based on this, we make choices in our life.

We only see things which we want to see in this world. If you want to see only negative, you will find this world full of negativity, pain and bad things only. But the moment you want to see magic in the universe, it will appear at every moment in your life. Never allow your heart to be filled with hatred, jealousy, complaints, etc. Replace them with compassion, vision and gratitude.

# 12

# Addressing the Issue

The first and foremost step in the process of healing is that you must become honest with yourself. This quality will not only help you heal but will also help you become one of the best versions of yourself.

Take a piece of paper and write down the names of people you don't ever want to see in your life again. These can be from any part of your life, such as your high school friend, your relative, your boss or your spouse. Now one by one think about what the reasons are that you never want to see them again, and why you have anger towards them.

This is what you have stored in your body, and now it is time to talk to each one of them mentally and thank them. It is because of them you were able to move ahead in life, as this is the law of karma. These people had karma to wake you up and challenge your inner core only for a few months or years in your life, and then they left. It was you who kept them stored in your body as the days passed.

This is a line from the Shanti Parva: *As two logs of wood floating in the great ocean come together and are again (when the time comes) separated, even so, creatures come together and are again (when the time comes) separated.*

These people were meant to be there only for a certain time period. Now you should continue your journey.

But if this person is still in your life, and it could be anyone, then you need to prepare yourself and get ready for the extreme. What I mean by extreme is to get ready to make decisions as your life is about to change. You cannot continue your life worrying that something wrong can happen. If you are afraid about your job or worried that your spouse doesn't like you anymore or you have a problem with your in-laws, all this is going to change.

You need to make a decision. It can be at either end, but you cannot be neutral. Look at countries that fought wars. The country that won World War II got a man on the moon, and the one that lost became a pioneer in technology. It is always winners and losers who count, not the people who sit on the sidelines and watch the world burn. Similarly, it is always the mad people who get up and do great work, not the ones who keep going on with life, bearing pressure.

Let me introduce you to a character named Chan. In 2011, I was on the sea in the Middle East, working as a sub-engineer on a critical project. The office gave us a choice that either the supervisor or the sub-engineer could do a crew change, but not both. This was important as it was the end of the project, and the new team would not be able to handle the change.

It was a matter of a maximum of ten days. My supervisor had to leave for Syria, so I took over his position. The person who was coming to replace him was Chan. The ROV (Remotely Operated Vehicles) industry is a very small industry and everyone knows everyone. Chan had a reputation for being abusive towards the team, throwing tools at team members, and getting angry without any reason whatsoever. Chan was difficult to deal with and everyone in the team knew this. He was able to get away with it as he was an old-timer in the industry and had many friends holding high positions in the office. Chan himself had started as a saturation diver and then later moved on to ROV. He had almost thirty-five to forty years of experience in the industry.

He was to arrive over the weekend. I was sitting with Jugaad Baba, the chief engineer of the ship. A man who was always smiling and full of wisdom. All day he sat on a chair and read books. You could approach him with any problem and even when he was half-drunk, he would have a solution for it. He had spent half his life on vessels. Jugaad Baba told me one beautiful line filled with wisdom, 'He is only angry to a point until you accept it.'

I nodded and said I would try. At night, the crew change was happening and I was sleeping in my bunk bed after my shift. As a rule, if your crew change happens at night, you should not disturb the crew sleeping and try to make minimum noise. I could hear Chan's loud footsteps in the room and his complaining about a towel not being provided and about so many other things. He was shouting at the housekeeping staff standing in the room, even though he knew that I was trying to sleep. At this point, I made up my mind. I got up from the bed and started shouting in a louder voice than him, telling him the rules about not entering a room when someone was sleeping.

It was a surprise for Chan, as he had never seen that reaction before from anyone, as no one had dared to stand up to him. I told him some beautiful words in French and I was so loud that the captain, who was next door, also came to see the verbal argument. The captain was not happy with Chan and his attitude, and told him to just shut up and let everyone sleep.

I went to bed and the next morning Chan apologized for his behaviour. During the whole trip, he behaved well with all the crew members. Now what do you think happened here? If I had not shouted at that point of time, during the whole trip I would have had to deal with Chan's bad behaviour. Sometimes, it is better to fight with full force so you can live peacefully for the rest of your life.

People take you for granted till they can. They will treat you the same way until you tell them to back off and tell them not to cross the line. If someone has wrong expectations, that is their fault, not yours. You need to be firm and tell people that every action has consequences and if you will not say this to their face, then next time be ready for the same behaviour to be repeated.

If your partner is having an extramarital affair and you are still stuck in the marriage, for whatever reason, the only person at fault is you. You are choosing to stay in an abusive relationship and are accepting it for whatever reason you think will justify it. I might sound blunt at this point, but once you accept a particular behaviour, the human tendency is to take it to the next level automatically.

You allow people to disrespect you as you have lost confidence within you. Otherwise, no one on this earth can disrespect you for any reason. You either enjoy the situation and give your 100 per cent and be committed to the work assigned to you or leave and do what makes you happy.

In every group, there are people who keep on complaining about so many things that are wrong, like their job, their partner or something else. But these people will not do anything to change the situation. If you have one of these people living inside you, throw them out now, as this is the person who is stopping you from becoming one of the happiest creatures on earth. Who is stopping you from changing this? It is worth trying every day, to strive for a better situation rather than accepting conditions as they are.

In case you have people around you who make excuses, complain or keep on telling you how difficult their life is, these are people who steal your energy and need to get out of your life. If someone has a problem in life, by all means, be compassionate, help them, but if someone is repetitive and keeps on whining about one thing or the other, then it is time for this person to be out of your life.

Once you start addressing the issues related to pain in your life, whether it is from the past or the present, then you will see that your energy will suddenly increase. Your vision towards your goal will become clear. Moreover, you can experience new energy in your life.

Scan QR code to access the
Penguin Random House India website